Lives of the Poet
The First Century of Keats Biography

Lives of the Poet
The First Century of Keats Biography

William Henry Marquess

The Pennsylvania State University Press
University Park and London

Library of Congress Cataloging in Publication Data

Marquess, William Henry.
Lives of the poet.

Includes bibliography and index.
1. Keats, John, 1795–1821—Biography—History.
2. Biography (as a literary form) 3. Poets,
English—19th century—Biography. I. Title.
PR4836.M37 1985   821'.7 [B]   84-43064
ISBN 0-271-00390-1

Copyright © 1985 The Pennsylvania State University

All rights reserved

Printed in the United States of America

For My Parents

Contents

	Acknowledgments	ix
	Prologue	1
1.	A Space of Life Between *The Context*	5
2.	A Continual Allegory *Keats's Autobiography*	15
3.	Strange Customs *Richard Monckton Milnes*	37
4.	Inheriting Unfulfilled Renown *Mid-Victorian Estimates*	59
5.	Among the English Poets *W. M. Rossetti and Sidney Colvin*	75
6.	The Sympathetic Imagination *Amy Lowell*	91
	Epilogue	109
	Notes	115
	Bibliography	125
	Index	131

Acknowledgments

My general debts are too numerous for recapitulation; I hope that all those who have encouraged me in this work will recognize my gratitude. Specific debts I acknowledge with pleasure. Walter Jackson Bate was not only the second reader of this study when it was a doctoral dissertation; his own work in literary biography, which combines scholarly probity with a warmhearted understanding of life, was its inspiration. Jerome Hamilton Buckley was the ideal first reader: he was always ready with careful criticism and generous encouragement, and his vast knowledge of Victorian culture guided me clear of more pitfalls than I care to admit. Henry C. Moses has given me a liberal education in intellectual honesty and good-humored commitment to principle; he had assistance from Morton Prince. Craig L. Thomas offered sturdy friendship and a living example of dedication to the teaching of literature. During the two years of research and writing, Alessandra Dini heartened me with *pazienza*, *forza*, and all the warmth of Tuscany. Finally, Joel A. Dando has lived with this project virtually as along as I have. It was his effortless charm, nine years ago, that first moved me to study Romantic poetry; his intelligence, wit, and abiding friendship have enriched my hours ever since. He questioned, criticized, and cheered this study from inception to completion; he believed in it when I did not; he was always, as Keats said of Shakespeare, its presiding genius. My debt to him is not the greatest only because it is not the first. The first and most enduring debt is inscribed in the dedication.

Prologue

> His art is happy, but who knows his mind?
> —Yeats, "Ego Dominus Tuus"

Reasons for studying biography need hardly be enumerated. The cult of personality that Coleridge identified is still with us, and, as the gossip tabloids continue to vulgarize the scrutiny of private lives, it is well to be mindful of the true uses of biography. Samuel Johnson, who loved the genre above all other kinds of literature, puts it best: "No species of writing seems more worthy of cultivation than biography, since none can be more delightful or useful, none can more certainly enchain the heart by irresistible interest, or more widely diffuse instruction to every diversity of condition."[1]

Biography deserves fresh attention today for more than its powerful capacity to achieve the classical ends of instruction and delight. As the novel grew to maturity in the nineteenth century, so biography has come into its own in the twentieth, following modern interest in individual psychology and profiting from improved standards and tools of scholarship. In fact, it is apparent that modern experimentation in the novel helped to raise biography from its traditional position as an adjunct of history. As modern novelists sought to refine their craft, exploring the most remote possibilities of presentation—distorting chronology or character, creating word-structures rather than telling stories—many readers turned to biography for the satisfactions of conventional narrative and the study of character in a recognizable human setting. Now that biography has taken its place as an intellectual pursuit somewhere in between history and the novel, a study of its own means and ends—comparable to historiography—is needed.

Such a study, in the abstract, is far beyond my present scope. As Lytton

Strachey might have said, the history of biography will never be written: we know too much about it. Instead, I have chosen, as a student of literature, to focus on literary biography, and, within that realm, to concentrate on a single case study. In defense of literary biographers, William Butler Yeats argued that a poet's life is "an experiment in living and those that come after have a right to know it."[2] I have limited my study of the development of biography to the lives of a single poet in the hope that it will add to our understanding of just such an experiment.

A new work on the life of John Keats may call for more in the way of justification. As early as 1925, Amy Lowell apologized for repeating what was already a "twice-told tale"; since then the story of Keats's life has been told many times over. I have chosen to focus on the development of that well-known story for three major reasons. First, Keats's life came at a crucial moment in the history of English biography. It allows us an opportunity to analyze the response of biographers to the example of Boswell, whose inimitable *Life of Johnson* was published in 1791, just four years before Keats's birth. Second, Keats's career is rich in questions that sparked controversy throughout the nineteenth and early twentieth centuries, making it a barometer of taste in biography. An obscure beginning; wounds suffered at the hands of Philistine critics; a passionate and pathetic romantic attachment; an early, pitiful death—this is the stuff of melodrama against which scholarly rigor may be measured. And finally, the fairy-tale quality of Keats's life simply continues to fascinate modern readers, as witnessed by the abundance of excellent biographical research completed in the past twenty years by such scholars as Walter Jackson Bate, Aileen Ward, and Robert Gittings. A study of the transmission of this moving story may help describe, in concrete and consistent terms, the development of literary biography in general.

The reader who desires a more universal treatment of that subject should repair to Richard D. Altick's compendious history, *Lives and Letters* (1965). Those interested in the more purely literary reception of Keats will profit from George Ford's *Keats and the Victorians* (1944) and G. M. Matthews's volume in the "Critical Heritage" series (1971). My study inevitably shares common points with both of those approaches, but attempts to steer a course between them, finding in the changing conceptions of Keats the man an illustration of the progress of biography, its methods and its aims.

As is inevitable with a work covering a great deal of material, much here has had to be summarized. In order to set the stage for a discussion of Keats biography, I begin this study with two chapters of an introductory nature. Chapter 1 evaluates the standards of biography in the first half of the nineteenth century, before the composition of the first full-scale life of Keats. Chapter 2 analyzes the autobiographical content of the poet's own writings—the biographers' raw materials. Thereafter the discussion focuses on particular biographies (Chapters 3, 5, and 6) and the development of a biographical image (Chapter 4), in roughly chronological order.

Although the past sixty years have witnessed a burgeoning of scholarship on Keats's life, this study ends with Amy Lowell's 1925 biography for several reasons. Lowell started her work as a lecture for the centennial of Keats's death, deliberately rounding off a century of posthumous attention to the poet. For all its flaws, her study is the first really "modern" biography of Keats, insofar as she knowingly suppressed none of her materials; it stands as a landmark for comparison to earlier works. After Lowell's massive effort, the biographical scholarship on Keats becomes so multiplicitous that generalizations about it are both more difficult and less valuable. Essentially, she and Sidney Colvin bring a close to the nineteenth-century view of the poet, the main concern of this book.

The chief danger of a study like this is that the poet himself may be lost in the accumulation of secondary accounts and scholarly disputes. John Masefield ruefully recorded this concern:

> When I am buried, all my thoughts and acts
> Will be reduced to lists of dates and facts,
> And long before this wandering flesh is rotten
> The dates which made me will be all forgotten;
> And none will know the gleam there used to be
> About the feast-days freshly kept by me,
> But men will call the golden hour of bliss
> "About this time," or "shortly after this."[3]

Of course, we cannot know, exactly, the gleam there was about Keats's days; it is irrecoverable now, a mere thing of words. But, though much is taken, much abides—in the poetry, to which we must always return; among the letters, in which we find his speaking voice; and in the efforts of biographers to interpret the remains. My hope is that in considering their attempts to know his mind we may better understand both the poet and his readers.

1
A Space of Life Between
The Context

Frown not, old ghosts, if I be one of those
Who make you utter things you did not say,
And mould you all awry and mar your worth;
For whatsoever knows us truly, knows
That none can truly write his single day,
And none can write it for him upon earth.
—Tennyson, Preface to "Becket"

When Richard Monckton Milnes took on the writing of the first full-scale life of Keats in 1841, modern English biography was still young. Boswell's *Life of Johnson*, which marks the beginning of modern biography, had been published just fifty years before. In many ways that half-century, which roughly coincides with the Romantic period in England, marked the beginning of the biographical practices that would be used by Victorians like Milnes. Keats himself offers a metaphor for the early growth of the genre, in his Preface to *Endymion*. "The imagination of a boy is healthy," he wrote, "and the mature imagination of a man is healthy; but there is a space of life between, in which the soul is in a ferment, the character undecided, the way of life uncertain."[1] Boswell, whose work represents the felicitous concurrence of talent, timing, and a compelling subject, is the healthy boy of English biography. His early nineteenth-century followers, who were sometimes cowed by his example, sometimes constrained by an Evangelical public, exemplify the growing pains of the young art. A brief survey of some biographical accounts that illustrate crises in the development of the genre may help us understand the methods at the disposal of nineteenth-century biographers of Keats, and better enable us to appreciate their attempts to decide the character of biography.

Before Boswell, the status of biography in English as an independent genre was doubtful at best: it was usually regarded as one of the minor auxiliaries of history. Until Johnson's *Rambler* Number 60, virtually no one had found the writing of lives worthy of prolonged consideration.[2] In essence, there were two types of lives at the time: formal panegyric, a descendant of hagiography; and the scurrilous journalistic briefs of "the Unspeakable" Edmund Curll, who made a reputation by destroying reputations. James Boswell was certainly not alone in transforming a dubious pursuit into a recognized form of art. He followed the theory of Johnson himself, whose compact "Lives" provided small-scale examples of critical biography, and he emulated the practice of William Mason, whose *Life of Gray* (1774) was the first to include many of its subject's letters as firsthand documentation. Moreover, he wrote in a time that was responding to the light that John Locke shed on individual behavior and ordinary experience, inspiring a new particularism and a rise of realism in fiction. John O. Lyons has called this moment in the growth of Western thought "the hinge of consciousness in the eighteenth century." Before the 1760s, he argues, most biographical or autobiographical writing was concerned with general truth, the universal condition of the Christian soul. After 1770, a variety of developments (such as political revolutions that nourished an awareness of change, and journalistic novels that considered life interesting for its own sake rather than for its moral lessons) inspired biographers to pay more attention to the inner lives of their subjects.[3] Making the most of these conditions, Boswell helped to promote biography from its previous role as handmaiden to history. Within fifty years, Thomas Carlyle could claim that all history was nothing more than "the essence of innumerable biographies."[4]

The Life of Johnson achieves its monumental effect for a host of reasons, not the least of which is a magnificent subject. Zealous note-taking, tenacious memory, dramatic sense, honest attention to fact (he bragged that he had "run half over London" to verify a date), and a lively personal style account for much of Boswell's success. But he was also a timely-happy spirit: appearing on the cusp between the eighteenth-century insistence on general, decorous truth and the nineteenth-century impulse toward individual, idiosyncratic truths, his "Flemish portrait" of Johnson manages to combine closely observed detail with the massive stateliness of the moralist's subject, the proper study of mankind. Recent studies of Boswell's personal papers show that in part he maintained decorum through the art of tactful omission: his notes include descriptions of apparent indiscretions (a story about an early drunken night, Johnson's reference to seeking a second wife not long after Tetty's death, Mrs. Desmoulins's hints about his amorous inclinations) that do not appear in the text.[5] His editing also struck out details about himself and other living figures, and he was probably saved from indiscretion about Johnson's darker secrets by the bliss of ignorance. Nonetheless, Boswell's practice of relatively full disclosure—his publication of private conversations, his relish of idiosyncratic detail such as Johnson's nervous tics, and his carefully directed dramatic scenes—established a paradigm for later biographers. In his carefully posed portrait of a great moralist, Boswell was clearly a chronicler of late eighteenth-century values. But in his bold aim "to Johnsonize the land," his stress on the significance of an eccentric individual, and his copious particularity, he sounded Romantic notes that biographers of the Romantic period were not always willing, or able, to play.

That the Romantic period, which Coleridge deprecated as an "age of personality," was fascinated by the lives of literary men is abundantly demonstrated by the spate of biographical works that followed Boswell's. Isaac D'Israeli, father of the future prime minister, capitalized on the vogue with his compilation entitled *The Literary Character* (1795), a compendium of literary figures and incidents. Lives of Dryden (by Malone, in 1800) and Chaucer (by Godwin, in 1803) indicate a vigorous interest in past classics, while more recent authors like Cowper (Hayley, 1803, and Southey, 1835) and Burns (Currie, 1800, and Cunningham, 1834) commanded unprecedented attention. Nor was the popularity of biography limited to scholarly works, as periodicals of the day overflowed with profiles and memoirs, from a series entitled "Portraits of Authors" in *The Champion* (1814) to DeQuincey's recollections of the Lake poets, published in *Tait*'s during the 1830s.

We must, however, exercise care in the application of the "Romantic" label to the biographical work of the period. First of all, we should expect that the poets with whom we associate the term, taking seriously their role as Shelleyan hierophants, would be ahead of scholars in the general movement toward the exaltation of the particular, the individual, and the idiosyncratic. It is no coincidence that of the three most highly regarded biographies of the period, two (Southey's *Nelson* and Moore's *Byron*) were written by noted poets and the third (Lockhart's *Scott*) by a novelist and critic who had ample contact with several major poets.

Even poets, though, were not sure that the new focus on detail ought to be extended to the writing of biography. Wordsworth, the champion of everyday life, real speech and real men, was the most outspoken in his objection to the "Boswellian plan." In his "Letter to a Friend of Robert Burns" (1816), which he had printed in order to broadcast his position, Wordsworth explained that biography is not a science, in which truth is "sought without scruple," merely because it is "serviceable"; rather, it is an art, which should be published "only for obviously justifying purposes, moral or intellectual." Wordsworth makes it clear that he is especially concerned with biographies of authors, who provide the only necessary personal record in their works, "without an admixture of useless, irksome, and painful details."[6] Given the poet's heavily weighted terms, only a Philistine could object: who else would prefer an irksome science to a justly moral art? The stance taken by Wordsworth, who became an established spokesman even as his poetry declined, suggests that the young nineteenth century's view of biography had not advanced as far from eighteenth-century practice as other changes might lead us to expect.

Indeed, it is apparent that many writers of the nineteenth century actually feared the application of the "Boswellian plan" to literary lives. Vicesimus Knox, a Tonbridge schoolmaster, wrote "On the Character of Doctor Johnson and the Abuse of Biography" in 1824, admitting, "I am apprehensive that the custom of exposing the nakedness of eminent men to every eye, will have an unfavourable influence on virtue. It may teach men to fear celebrity; and, by extinguishing the desire of fame and posthumous glory, destroy one powerful motive to excellence."[7] In this sense, Boswell's very success may have contributed to arresting the development of candid biography: now that famous authors could expect to be scrutinized by aspiring biographers, they were more likely to watch their words and gestures with caution. A midcentury reviewer summarized "the terrors of biography" by sympathizing with its subjects: "Were we placed in such a trying position, we should utter, before our intending Boswell, nothing save sentiments which might have flowed from the lips of the Venerable Bede."[8] This reaction to *The Life of Johnson* did not have a specific influence on the lives of Keats, who never achieved enough celebrity to fear that a biographer would bother to reveal his secrets. But it did affect the standards of biography that Monckton Milnes inherited: the period immediately following Boswell, rendered unusually self-conscious by his example, seldom sought Romantic particularism and exploration of the inner life in biography.

In fact, the term "Romantic biography" is useful primarily as a chronological handle. Biographers of the period were as equivocal in their response to Boswell's indecorous use of details as writers were wary of exposing themselves to his followers.[9] In general, biographical practice in the period was already closer to what we, in our grossly simplified adoption of broad terms, might call "Victorian"—earnest, exemplary, and overstuffed —than "Romantic" in the direction that Boswell had pointed.[10]

Most of the discussion of biographical practice in the early nineteenth century boils down to a controversy over the use of documentary materials like letters and journals. Boswell's employment of the "Mason method," publishing personal writings that would help carry his narrative, established a standard with which later biographers would have to reckon.[11] The practice was soon extended by lesser biographers like William Hayley, who presented his study of Cowper as little more than an autobiography constructed from the poet's correspondence. Such a method accorded with at least one major Romantic premise: implying a distrust of the biographer's "meddling intellect," it allowed direct access to the poetic genius itself. As a means of engaging the reader in judgment of the subject's most authentic self—present in his own words—it was to be claimed by biographers throughout the century, including Richard Monckton Milnes. But, for a variety of reasons, the writers of the best lives of the early nineteenth century found the so-called "epistolary autobiography" unsatisfactory.

Robert Southey presents an example. In his review of Hayley's *Cowper*, he rejects the practice of mere compilation. "It will seldom be employed," he predicts, "unless where the biographer is conscious of a paucity of materials for his own work, or of some nice and delicate points in the story, upon which he does not choose to express himself with the responsibility of an author."[12] Southey's chief criterion for biographical composition is apparent: it is the responsibility of the biographer to offer an interpretation of his materials. His own most famous work, the stirring *Life of Nelson* (1814), exemplifies his approach. Choosing not to provide the massive documentation of which nineteenth-century biography was to be so fond, Southey condensed the busy life of Nelson into a vigorously paced story of heroism that he hoped would become "a manual for the young sailor."[13] His technique for achieving such brevity relies on the artistic freedom to focus a narrative by fixing upon a principle—here, Nelson's high sense of honor. (This method is appropriate, of course, for a subject who is a man of action rather than of letters. The "Life and Letters" may be a more useful format for the biography of a writer, whose inner life, as revealed in correspondence, usually demands more attention.) Southey illustrates his hero's stern devotion to honor with artfully chosen leitmotifs. The young officer's intuition collides several times with conventional naval wisdom, and he disobeys orders, refusing to compromise his integrity; determined to be a hero from the time of his first teenage bout with malaria, he intermittently expresses a tragic death wish (keeping a prize coffin in his quarters); finally, he refuses to follow the advice of his colleagues to stay below deck at Trafalgar, even though—or, as Southey suggests, because—he suspects that it must be his last battle. These recurrent dramatic touches lend the narrative a unity of action, in the tragic formula, that no mere compilation could provide.

A decision to highlight certain features, however, usually entails the obscuring of others. Southey's *Life of Nelson* demonstrates a classic problem for the biographer who desires to make a moral ideal of his subject: faced with facts that do not coincide with his image, he must either twist them or ignore them. Southey's presentation of Nelson involves both kinds of distortion. The overwhelming fact that he could not reconcile with his Man of Honor was Nelson's adulterous liaison with Emma Hamilton; the affair was widely known by 1800, when Lady Nelson separated from him. Aware of the futility of concealing the relationship, Southey tries to turn it to his own uses. First, he regrets that Emma became more than a friend, but reports that there was nothing "criminal" in their more-than-friendship (II, 42). (Southey's idea of "criminality" is hard to decipher: he later is compelled to imply, without stating outright, a fact by then well known—that Emma had secretly borne Nelson's child.) Then, to complicate matters, he explains that Nelson's apparently dishonorable behavior in an episode at Naples in 1800 (in Southey's account, he violated a truce flag and executed a patriot) was "influenced by an infatuated attachment" (II, 52) to the wife of the British consul there, Lady Hamilton. Thus the liaison with Emma, which Southey never concedes as a fact, becomes part of a morality play, in which Honor is the favorable wind that leads Nelson to victory, and Sex is at best an unlucky star, temporarily distracting him to treacherous shoals. Of course, the fact that Lady Hamilton was still alive when Southey wrote the biography doubtless affected his design as well; even if he had possessed all the letters relating to the affair (many of which were published in a scandalous edition in 1815) he would not have wanted to weave them into an "autobiography" that would wound her at the same time that it undermined his image of the hero. Monckton Milnes, writing long before the death of Fanny Brawne, would face the same problem.

Another reason for the unacceptability of the purely epistolary method of biography in the early nineteenth century is amply illustrated by Thomas Moore's study of Byron. The title alone indicates the biographer's desire for self-effacement: *Letters and Journals of Lord Byron*, proclaims the title page, then adds the afterthought, *With Notices of His Life*. And, in fact, the book comes to life largely because Moore had the good sense to allow Byron to present "his very self and voice" as often and as directly as possible. But of course full disclosure of Byron's often bawdy or irreligious descriptions of recent episodes and living persons was simply not possible, given contemporary standards of decency and the strictness of English libel laws. After losing his struggle to save the infamous memoirs, Moore printed virtually all that he could, with asterisks and ellipses veiling a multitude of unnamable names and presumably insalubrious byways. In fact, he employs a revealing double standard: he suppresses material only on Byron's premarital "affairs of gallantry" in England. Once the poet has arrived in Italy, he explains, "We have . . . shifted the scene to a region where less caution is requisite," allowing him to include, "with but little suppression, the noble poet's letters relative to his Italian adventures."[14] Clearly, the principle operating here is not a concern for decorum at all costs. Moore recognized that candor was truest to Byron's spirit; he also knew that the result could be legally actionable in England.

But Moore's presentation of Byron's letters and journals also demonstrates a subtler principle. The example of Boswell's *Johnson* inspired dread among authors who preferred not to have their private laundry hung on a public line. Dickens, Swinburne, and Hardy are among the nineteenth-century writers who burned what correspondence they could; surely others took care not to reveal too much in the first place, rendering exceedingly tenuous the assumption that a man is best known through his letters. Even if we discount the fear of Boswellian recording angels, that assumption was always doubtful. Letters are written in particular moods to particular recipients, about topics that later readers may not grasp; without the leavening of biographical commentary, they may disappoint or deceive the common reader. As Tennyson wrote in a sonnet that his son later printed in the preface of a singularly unrevealing biography of the poet,

> There lies the letter, but it is not he
> As he retires into himself and is:
> Sender and sent-to go to make up this,
> Their offspring of this union.[15]

Besides, letters mean different things to different writers. Keats, for instance, clearly turned to his correspondence as an outlet for most of his deepest concerns; Tennyson, who preferred to express himself in verse, declared that he would "as soon kill a pig as write a letter."[16]

Byron's epistolary performance provokes this discussion because, as is often the case, he presents an exception to the rule. Though some writers dreaded being "Boswellized," Byron clearly relished the prospect—both because he enjoyed playing a variety of roles and because his confessional impulse, everywhere evident in the poetry, was irrepressible. In providing Moore with memoirs, sometimes as he wrote them, Byron was not only generously helping his friend, who could solve some financial worries by getting an advance from the publisher for the posthumous edition of them; to some extent, he was also playing Prospero to Moore's Ariel, all but writing the biography himself. He knew, for instance, that the more conventional Moore was troubled by his subject's apparent dalliances with immorality, such as the irreligion of *Cain*, the liaison with Lady Caroline Lamb, and his friendship with the outspoken atheist Shelley.[17] But instead of concealing these blemishes from his future biographer, he undoubtedly took pleasure in exaggerating them, making Moore's task of explaining such behavior even more difficult. Although Moore's arch-Romantic explanation—that all of Byron's contradictions and waywardnesses were simply effusions of the mysterious breed called Genius—is too facile, his lucid and sympathetic commentary provides the necessary context for a mass of intractable but fascinating materials. Without it, the letters and journals, riddled as they had to be with omissions, would have been simply baffling. Like Monckton Milnes (and all of Keats's biographers), Moore was older than his subject would ever live to be, and he naturally took a protective stance towards the "hot youth" revealed in his materials.

A final example of the way that early nineteenth-century biography responded to Boswell and his imitators by adapting their methods is evident in John Gibson Lockhart's *Life of Scott* (1837–38). Where Southey had rejected the epistolary technique and Moore had adopted it with the care of an older friend who knew that he could not apply it indiscriminately, Lockhart both resisted the example of Boswell and applied it to his own ends.

The Life of Scott makes explicit the epstemological question that is raised but unstated in Moore's *Byron*: no matter how much contact we may have with a biographical subject, or how much memorabilia we may have from him, how can we really know him, "as he retires into himself and is"? Lockhart's answer is characteristically reticent. After recounting his first meeting with Scott in 1818, he explains why his portrait will not be as intimate as the reader might hope. "I never thought it lawful," he writes, "to keep a journal of what passes in private society, so that no one need expect from the sequel of this narrative any detailed record of Scott's familiar talk."[18] One of the great successes of particularity in *The Life of Johnson*, of course, is Boswell's uncanny re-creation of his hero's familiar talk. Lockhart, by contrast, simply refuses to "*Boswellize* Scott," explaining that the dangers of misrepresentation are too great. We may see, in this resistance to the one accepted classic of English biography, an attempt by Lockhart to shake off an intimidating example. But it is also apparent that in his recognition of the difficulties of understanding interlocutors' common assumptions, interpreting their intentions, and capturing their tones of voice, he raises questions of method that hardly gave Boswell pause. Near the end of his 900,000-word chronicle, he explains the basis of his doubt: "I distrust, even in very humble cases, our capacity for judging our neighbour fairly" (VII, 397). When surveying the life of an artist, he concludes, "It becomes, I can never help believing, modest understandings to rest convinced that there remained a world of deeper mysteries to which the dignity of genius would refuse any utterance" (VII, 398).

As an alternative to the Boswellian recording of private conversation and other privileged information available to him as the son-in-law of his subject, Lockhart proposes to return to an extreme form of the "Mason method"—that is, by publishing parts of letters and journals, "to extract and combine the scattered fragments of an *autobiography*" (V, 178). "It was my wish," he explains at the end, "to let the character develop itself: and conscious that I have wilfully withheld nothing that might assist the mature reader to arrive at just conclusions, I am by no means desirous of drawing out a detailed statement of my own" (VII, 398). He has turned Southey's practice upside down.

But the extraction and combination of "scattered fragments," of course, can amount to a detailed statement. Twentieth-century scholars have documented Lockhart's editorial infidelities at considerable length.[19] We now know that he sometimes altered Scott's language, that he moved passages from one letter to another or telescoped two letters together, that he shifted some of the blame for financial ruin away from his hero, and softened the evidence of Scott's final mental deterioration. It even seems likely that he invented some scenes with his novelist's touch, including a pious deathbed exhortation to the attendant son-in-law. Readers who are quick to sniff out evidence of "Victorian" concealment have not failed to cite Lockhart's own forlorn remark about his little deceptions: "The perhaps dismalest thing for me," he wrote to his publisher Robert Cadell in the midst of composition (20 June 1836), "is that very likely, when all his letters are thrown open to an unscrupulous after age, my manipulation may be thrown overboard entirely."[20]

An unscrupulous after-age has arrived, but it need not put the worst interpretation on Lockhart's "manipulation." The most capacious explanation is, as Francis R. Hart suggests, that his motivation was as much "Romantic" as it was "Victorian."[21] In essence, he wanted to combine two conflicting ideals of early nineteenth-century biography: imaginative sympathy and compendious particularity. Like Southey, he longed to preserve an image that would operate almost as a symbol—that of Scott as a man of dignity who fought tremendous odds to maintain his "stainless reputation." But he was also trying to let that character reveal itself in an organic way, through the compilation of Scott's own words. Thomas Moore had fought shy of the same goal, finding that social standards and an elusive subject would not allow its perfect realization. By comparison, Lockhart's infidelities were imposed on him only in part from the outside: several of Scott's close friends read his manuscript and requested changes of language and emphasis that he felt unable to refuse. His other willful inaccuracies are evidence of admirable intentions—to sustain a compelling narrative and to create an enduring image of a man he revered—that modern scholarship finds it difficult to accept. As we shall see, the efforts of the subsequent century to fix a biographical image of Keats are strewn with such intentions. Like Southey and Moore, Lockhart responded to the challenges of post-Boswellian biography with imperfect success. It is no wonder that Carlyle declared, in the midst of this period, that "a well-written life is almost as rare as a well-spent one."[22] The character of the genre was as yet undecided.

The first full-scale life on John Keats, published ten years after *The Life of Scott*, would have to wrestle with many of the questions raised by the preceding biographies. How does the biographer impose artistic order on a life, as Southey had done, without violating the essentially inartistic truth of life's vagaries? What does he do when, like Moore, he inherits a script that includes both a many-sided actor and unplayable scenes? When should he allow himself to dramatize or edit creatively, à la Lockhart, given a central idea that is not always supported by the available materials? Finally, where does he draw the lines between the private man and the public image, between discretion and the impulse to tell the whole truth, between the demands of living associates and the needs of posterity? Focusing on the lives of Keats, I intend to analyze the answers that a century of biographical scholarship has proposed to these questions. Now that we have considered some of the methods in practice at the time when Monckton Milnes undertook the first biography of Keats, let us turn to the materials of his story.

2
A Continual Allegory
Keats's Autobiography

Tel arbre, tel fruit.
    —Sainte-Beuve, "Chateaubriand"

When John Keats died in a Roman pensione at the age of twenty-five, he was, beyond a small group of friends and literati, virtually unknown. Unlike Byron and Shelley, he lacked the aura of high birth, material wealth, or a sensational public stance; unlike Wordsworth and Coleridge, he never attained the sagelike status of elder statesman; unlike almost all of his Romantic contemporaries, he seldom wrote about his autobiographical pilgrimage, or the moods of his own mind. Wordsworth brooded over his youth at length in *The Prelude*, and Coleridge recorded an impersonal literary life in the *Biographia*; Byron in his poetry created several autobiographical selves, and in his talk encouraged some of his contemporaries to create others, while Shelley made his own eccentric career a *cause célèbre*. Keats, partly because of his brief and relatively obscure life, partly because of his temperament, left no such prominent autobiographical record. In search of primary material in the poet's own words, the biographer of Keats must turn to his letters and to poems not avowedly autobiographical.

    The limited scope of Keats's writings about himself is not, however, in all respects a limitation. If he did not live long enough to cast a backward glance over travelled roads, neither did he have time to alter, embroider, misremember, or omit, as autobiographers often do in the attempt to produce a life that reads well. Virtually everything that we have from Keats's hand is fresh and immediate, giving the impression of work in progress. The letters are full of life and speculation on it, and the poems are rich with the ore of his dearest concerns. We cannot expect, of course, to find all that we look for in a full-dress autobiography: we miss the retrospective view and the consequent sense of design that an older writer might impose. Still, in order to evaluate the biographies that were to come later, we must first examine the autobiographical content of Keats's own writings. "Every secret of a writer's soul," wrote Virginia Woolf, "every experience of his life, every quality of his mind is written large in his works."[1] Keats himself agreed. "A Man's life of any worth is a continual allegory," he wrote to his brother and sister-in-law, "Shakspeare led a life of Allegory; his works are the comments on it."[2]

The primary source of autobiographical commentary in the works of Keats is the famous letters, which have been so extensively scrutinized, regretted, and applauded as to become a fundamental part of the poet's legend. Richard Monckton Milnes included about eighty of them (in varying states of wholeness and reliability, as we shall see) in his biography (1848), considering them "the best records of his outer existence."[3] In fact, in his effort to allow the letters to "tell their own tale," Milnes proposed to be no more than the editor of a posthumous autobiography; but the limitations of his resources (we now know of more than two hundred and fifty letters by Keats) too often required him to leave gaps in the narrative.

One of those gaps was filled spectacularly thirty years later, when Harry Buxton Forman published Keats's letters to Fanny Brawne, whose name had been discreetly withheld by Milnes. The controversy that these passionate love letters stirred is the well-known substance of a later chapter, in which I will examine Victorian canons of decorum; suffice it to say here that their publication caused such prominent figures as Matthew Arnold and Algernon Charles Swinburne to hesitate and reconsider their high estimates of Keats's character. Sidney Colvin, an important editor and biographer of Keats, was troubled by his "extreme unreserve" and continued to omit the letters to Fanny Brawne from his own editions of the letters long after they were well known, because, he said, they gave the reader "a sense of eavesdropping, of being admitted into petty private matters with which he has no concern."[4]

By the early twentieth century the furor over the love letters had subsided. In fact, Amy Lowell, thoroughgoing modernist that she was, meant to expose the corseted prudery of her Victorian predecessors by declaring that the letters were positively heroic.[5] But even without such a Romantic rereading, the twentieth century has generally rated Keats's epistolary achievement highly: T. S. Eliot claimed that the letters were "certainly the most notable and the most important ever written by any English poet,"[6] and biographers continue to turn to them as the most fruitful and reliable source for their work.

To say that Keat's letters constitute a natural resource for the understanding of his life is not, of course, to claim that he has written the autobiography for us, and that we need only disregard the postmarks and the salutations. Just such an attempt, compiled by Earle V. Weller in 1933 (and wishfully entitled *Autobiography of John Keats*), demonstrates the essential failings of the letters as autobiography. Naturally, the poet's childhood and youth pose problems: no letters written by Keats before his twentieth birthday remain, making an immediate "autobiographical" account of the early years impossible. Furthermore, the letters that have survived are seldom retrospective. Although we know that he was firmly attached to his siblings, for instance, Keats never mentions his parents or early family life. It may be argued that this omission represents a deliberate suppression of unhappy memories, leading the biographer to conclusions about Keats's youth. Indeed, the absence of reference to his difficult early years seems typical of a certain stoicism in his character: having lost his father at age eight and his mother at age fourteen, he preferred not to dwell on a painful time. But all this is biographical speculation, not autobiography. Considering how vividly childhood memories figure in the personal accounts of writers like Wordsworth and Ruskin, we do damage to the term "autobiography" if we apply it to a collection of letters that represents the final fifth of a poet's life.

The silence of the first twenty years is not the only problem facing the scholar who would ghostwrite Keats's autobiography. Even for the last five years of his life the epistolary record is far from complete. Hyder Edward Rollins, the authoritative editor of the letters, has identified from internal evidence some seventy letters of Keats that have been lost,[7] and of course there must have been many others for which we have no record at all. Keats himself, displaying remarkable disregard for future biographers, at least once made "a general conflagration of all old Letters and Memorandums" (letter to Sarah Jeffrey, 31 May 1819), possibly including some he himself had written. (This rash gesture came at a difficult time, when Keats was considering the abandonment of his cherished hopes for a poetic career in favor of more practical work. It does not indicate a general disregard or fastidiousness about his correspondence, which was dear to him, as he rejoiced in the exchange of ideas and feelings with his circle of friends.) Among the letters that remain, many survive only in copies, made by friends and correspondents, thus creating formidable textual problems. For instance, Charles Brown, a close friend who wrote one of the early memoirs of Keats, included in it nine letters, eight of which are otherwise unknown. Perhaps because he was so close to all the members of the small group Rollins has called "the Keats circle," Brown was careful to delete the names of many persons mentioned. In a letter of 22 September 1819, in which Keats is explaining why he should not go to live with Brown at Hampstead, we have this transcription: "I like xxxxxxxxx and I cannot help it. On that account I had better not live there." If we did not otherwise know that Fanny Brawne was then living at Hampstead, we might find the identity—even the gender—of "xxxxxxxxx" most perplexing; and, in fact, some of Brown's blanks have not been satisfactorily filled.

An old friend's discretion is only one of several reasons for textual difficulties in the letters. Another highly uncertain copyist was John Jeffrey, the second husband of Georgiana Keats, John's sister-in-law. He reported to Milnes that he had transcribed "nearly all" of Keats's letters to his brother and Georgiana, including the crucial long journal letters of 1819. But comparison of his copies with recovered originals shows how little he cared for the project: changing and omitting freely, he reduced one thirty-four-page letter to a three-page "copy" for the biographer.[8] Lest this editorial accounting seem trivial, it should be noted that among the letters surviving only in Jeffrey's transcription is the famous passage on "Negative Capability" (letter to George and Tom Keats, 21, 27 December 1817), which has become a standard concept in our critical vocabulary. That letter itself is a case study in the unreliability of these texts: Jeffrey dated it December 1818, instead of 1817; he omitted at least two passages of unknown length, writing simply "&&" to indicate one ellipsis and leaving the chronology of the letter askew at the other; and he seems to have miscopied words, writing, for instance, that Coleridge would let go by "a fine insolated verisimilature" where we suspect that Keats wrote "isolated verisimilitude." Keats's own spelling is uncertain enough without such confusions. Other examples of textual problems abound, but it is sufficient to say that we simply cannot know exactly what Keats wrote in some of the letters. All of these circumstances render it difficult to make accurate biography of the letters, much less autobiography.

The textual difficulties also suggest something fundamentally inadequate about the letters of Keats (and most other letters) as autobiography. It is apparent, from the uncorrected errors, the casual flights from topic to topic, and the rapidity with which he answered some letters written to him, that Keats usually wrote his letters quickly and spontaneously. This is not to say that none of them is profoundly reflective; in fact, they are rife with speculation on the nature of poetry and life—two subjects that he was loath to separate. But even Keats's deepest meditation, like the passage on the "Vale of Soul-making" to George and Georgiana (14 February–3 May 1819), seems to grow casually out of his everyday experience, often out of random reading. Although he is always tenderly conscious of his own position—both as a poet in the English tradition and as a person in English society—there is never in the letters a systematic effort at self-evaluation, seldom a judgment of deeds done. He characteristically writes of the present and the future, of poetics and projects to come. This lack of retrospection is natural, of course: letters tend to be current rather than reminiscent. Some writers, like Byron, often look back in their letters, hoping to reinterpret, recapture, or even reshape the past. Keats, though, is more like the instinctive animal he describes in a letter to his brother and sister-in-law (19 March 1819): "The Creature has a purpose and his eyes are bright with it."

The purpose, of course, is to communicate with a particular correspondent. This essential function of letter-writing—addressing a limited, specific audience—also distinguishes it from the general declarations of autobiography. Whereas the autobiographer would dress his life in public utterance in order to impress an unknown "common reader," or even an especially literate reader, Keats is writing quite personally to an uncommonly close circle of friends and his three beloved younger siblings, going out to them individually, putting in practice what in poetry he called "a greeting of the Spirit" with its object. Keats has long been admired for his capacity for sympathetic identification in his poetry, following the aesthetic theory of Hazlitt—that is, his disinterested ability (or "negative capability") to leave subjective concerns behind and identify with the object he contemplates. This characteristic is frequently manifest in the letters, and it can create problems for the biographer, who may have trouble pinning down the "Camelion poet." When Keats writes to Benjamin Robert Haydon, the boldly dramatic painter, he is breathless, full of fire and hope, planning to "attack" his work; when writing to the jaunty and sociable poet Leigh Hunt he is usually witty and alusive, signing with the alias "Junkets"; and to John Hamilton Reynolds, a contemporary poet and perhaps his closest friend, he sends some of his deepest speculation on poetry and philosophy, including the famous letter on "the Chamber of Maiden-Thought." This multiplicity of tone does not mean that Keats self-servingly changed his voice to suit his audience; it means that he met his particular correspondents on particular grounds, as we all do, with an especially imaginative—and not always conscious—sensitivity to their individuality. It also means that the biographer must take care not to assume that any particular statement in the letters is factually reliable, as the correspondent and the circumstances must always be evaluated along with the statement. This is a point where the failure of Weller's so-called "Autobiography" of Keats is especially acute: in order to create the impression of a work of continuous prose, Weller has deleted salutations and signatures, changed pronouns, and removed personal asides from the letters so that they read like a seamless journal. In the process, he has drained from them much of their life and compelling personal interest. It may yet be possible to extract the autobiographical content from the letters of Keats, but we will need more tools than scissors and paste.

One last and crucial consideration must be added to this catalogue of the limitations of Keats's letters as autobiography: Keats's character itself. Although he was generally a frank, unguarded correspondent, he could be reticent on certain subjects, as we have already seen in the absence of reference to his parents. In the face of personal loss—which he knew too well—he was almost always stoic. When his brother George planned to depart for America in 1818, leaving John to care for their consumptive brother Tom alone, Keats characteristically did not mention it in his letters for weeks.[9] Later, as he sat by Tom's deathbed, he contrived to entertain his distant brother and sister-in-law by writing a fanciful lullaby to their as-yet unborn first child, expressing the hope that it would become "the first American poet." Such self-containment in times of adversity is yet another reason why we cannot expect to find complete self-revelation in the letters.

Still, for all these warnings about the limitations of reading Keats's letters as autobiography, they remain full of autobiographical content that is invaluable in forming any evaluation of the man. It may be helpful here to consider what parts of the Keats story we know primarily from the letters alone.

First, there are Keats's aesthetic beliefs, however inchoate they may be. Without the letters, we would know nothing of negative capability, or of the unobtrusive "poetical character," as distinguished from "the wordsworthian or egotistical sublime" (letter to Richard Woodhouse, 27 October 1818). It is in a letter to his publisher John Taylor (27 February 1818) that Keats explains that poetry should "surprise by a fine excess and not by Singularity," and that it should come "as naturally as the Leaves to a tree" or not at all. And to Shelley he wrote (16 August 1820) that an artist must have "self-concentration," must " 'load every rift' of [his] subject with ore." In short, Keats's poetic axioms (they are hardly so systematic as to be called a body of theory) are found almost entirely in brief, casual passages of the letters. This observation might not seem autobiographically significant; yet in Keats's short life so many things are of a piece that it would be wrong to separate aesthetics from character. It is typical that the axioms should be sown intermittently through the letters, because Keats was not a "consequitive" thinker, as he called some of his more theoretical colleagues. And these casual comments on poetry are also biographically important because they amount to an ethical ideal. The goal of negative capability, with all that it implies about the rejection of Romantic egoism, the willingness to lose oneself in something larger or more meaningful, and the ability to empathize with others, is critical to the understanding of Keats's character.

These aesthetic concerns are naturally interwoven in the letters with a second matter of biographical importance, Keats's philosophical speculations. Again, he is not by nature a theorist: he would never have written a philosophical treatise, and, although the poetry surely reflects his metaphysical concerns, it would be critically disastrous to consider any single poem as a program for certain beliefs. But he was a thinker, and his letters announce most of his deepest thoughts, usually months before they find their way into the poetry. In an early letter (to Benjamin Bailey, 22 November 1817), for instance, Keats cries, "O for a Life of Sensations rather than of Thoughts!" This apparently arch-Romantic call, raising the value of intuitive perception over the "false secondary power" of reason that Wordsworth describes, has occasioned endless commentary by critics who would see it as a credo. In fact, it is a lighthearted interjection that comes in the midst of provocative thinking about the imagination; Keats went on to refine and modify it throughout the letters and poems, as his experience of the world accumulated. To be sure, the letters are essential to a study of Keats's thought (and thus to the biography); but it must be remembered, as Keats himself admitted in the middle of one of his most profoundly thoughtful letters (to George and Georgiana, 19 March 1819), that he was young, "writing at random—straining at particles of light in the midst of a great darkness."

A third important part of Keats's character that we know largely through the letters is his sense of humor. Too often (especially after discussions like the one above) our impression is that of an exceedingly earnest young man, preoccupied by family ties and financial worries, spouting poetry and poetics. Indeed, he had reason to worry about his worldly circumstances, and his seriousness about the poetic calling sometimes approached religious devotion, especially in the early days. Moreover, the poetry contains little that is really comic: his one sustained satiric effort, *The Jealousies, or The Cap and Bells*, is universally recognized as a failure. The letters show, however, that Keats possessed a lively sense of humor, sprightly, clever, and occasionally salty. Comic interludes in Keats's letters almost always involve fanciful wordplay, and often arise from his empathic ability to put himself in the place of someone (or something) else. In a letter to Reynolds (3 February 1818) which goes on to posit serious speculation about modern poetry, he begins, "Would we were a sort of ethereal Pigs, & turn'd loose to feed upon spiritual Mast & Acorns—which would be merely being a squirrel & feed[ing] upon filberts. for what is a squirrel but an airy pig, or a filbert but a sort of archangelical acorn?" Writing to Benjamin Bailey about the wet climate and the weak countrymen of Devonshire (13 March 1818), he explains:

> The hills are very beautiful, when you get a sight of 'em—the Primroses are out, but then you are in—the Cliffs are of a fine deep Colour, but then the Clouds are continually vieing with them. . . . The native men are the poorest creatures in England. . . . Had England been a large devonshire we should not have won the Battle of Waterloo. . . . A Devonshirer standing on his native hills is not a distinct object—he does not show against the light.

The variety of tone that is often evident in a single letter of Keats—he may move from comedy to melancholy to meditation in the space of a long paragraph—reflects the leading characteristics of his humor. One is the quicksilver of his mind and his situation: the letters display him as a young man of extraordinarily flexible spirit adjusting daily to shifting circumstances. Thus, in the letter to Bailey cited above he segues from comic scorn for Devonshire ("I wonder I meet with no born Monsters") to doubt about his chosen career ("I am sometimes so very sceptical as to think Poetry itself a mere Jack a lanthern") to poetic contemplation of "Things real—things semireal—and no things" ("every mental pursuit takes its reality and worth from the ardour of the pursuer"). And the missive ends with unexpected pathos when the world intrudes: "My Brother Tom desires to be remember'd to you—he has just this moment had a spitting of blood poor fellow." Such fluidity of thought can make it difficult to characterize Keats's mood for any extended period; as he says in the same letter on the variability of the mind, "We take but three steps from feathers to iron."

Another trait evident in the variety of Keats's epistolary tone is his habit of using humor to cover or put the best face on difficult situations. It is apparent, for instance, that throughout the visit to Devonshire in the spring of 1818 he was ill at ease—preoccupied by Tom's illness and worried about his future as a poet, while George was clearly growing restless about his own career. Keats releases tension—and tries to conceal real concern—by humorously taking it out on the weather (describing the County's "urinal qualifications" although he had been "peedisposed" to like it) and sharing earthy jests with James Rice ("some of the little Barmaids look'd at me as if I knew Jem Rice"). Thus even Keats's vital sense of humor mixes almost always with his essential reticence and stoicism; to the end, on the desperate voyage to Italy, he continued to crack jokes and puns with Severn and fellow travellers.

The fact that Keats's humor is seldom far from some touch of pathos, however, should not obscure the animal good spirits that might have shone through more brightly in happier circumstances. As letters tend to be written in quiet, private moments, they do not reveal all of the writer's capacity for conviviality. Keats himself explains this phenomenon (to George and Georgiana, 20 September 1819), using a conversational style that hints of his own good-natured presence:

> Writing has this disadvan[ta]ge of speaking. one cannot write a wink, or a nod, or a grin, or a purse of the Lips, or a *smile—O law*! One can-[not] put ones finger to one's nose, or yerk ye in the ribs, or lay hold of your button in writing—but in all the most lively and titterly parts of my Letter you must not fail to imagine me as the epic poets say—now here, now there, now with one foot pointed at the ceiling, now with another—now with my pen on my ear, now with my elbow in my mouth—O my friends you loose the action—and attitude is every thing as Fusili said when he took up his leg like a Musket to shoot a Swallow just darting behind his shoulder.

Even at the end of what is perhaps his most profound letter (to George and Georgiana, 14 February–3 May 1819), after discussing his idea of the "Vale of Soul-making" and then copying out the first of the great odes, Keats is capable of a lightly self-deprecating touch, leavening the heavy speculation: "Here endethe ye Ode to Psyche." The biographical profile would be much less charming without these epistolary grace notes. As we shall see, Keats's nineteenth-century biographers would omit most of them, finding such frivolity unworthy of the high seriousness required of a real poet.

Finally, a fourth dimension of Keats that the letters make clear is that of the lover. The letters to Fanny Brawne are notorious and indispensable. We could, of course, draw conclusions about Keats's passionate character from the poems, some of them addressed to Fanny. But the development and the full extent of his romantic agony is known only from the letters. Here too, though, caution must be exercised, lest the biographer be dazzled by the intensity of those last letters and construct scandalous generalizations, as some Victorian readers were all too willing to do. We must not train the sensationally white light of a brief, specific, diseased period on an entire life and character. The love letters surely are not autobiographical, in the sense that an older, calmer, healthier Keats would have retained them for inclusion in his own story; but they remain crucial documents of the final year, and they may serve as a test of the biographer's ability to comprehend and embrace all the parts of a various man.

"A Man in love I do think cuts the sorryest figure in the world," Keats wrote to George and Georgiana in September 1819. This is not necessarily true, as we know, for instance, from the generously persistent comportment of Robert Browning in his letters to Elizabeth Barrett. But here, as so often in his acutely self-conscious letters, Keats is the best judge of his own character. He could not bear the public spectacle of swooning lovers, as he described them in light verse to George and Georgiana:

> Pensive they sit, and roll their languid eyes,
> Nibble their toasts, and cool their tea with sighs,
> Or else forget the purpose of the night,
> Forget their tea—forget their appetite.

But he knew already, writing this letter almost a year after meeting Fanny Brawne, that he was himself inclined to the melodramatic in romance, although he eschewed such public expression of it; in fact, it seems likely that his aversion to the sorry figure of the pathetic lover grew in defensive reaction to his own tendencies. In the earliest surviving letter to Fanny, written from self-imposed exile on the Isle of Wight, Keats begins with a self-restraining note: "I am glad I had not an opportunity of sending off a Letter which I wrote for you on Tuesday night—'twas too much like one out of Ro[u]sseau's Heloise. I am more reasonable this morning" (1 July 1819).

Still, even in his "more reasonable" mood, Keats reveals himself as the passionate lover who later troubled some Victorian readers. Soon after applauding his own restraint, he becomes self-pitying—"I have never known any unalloy'd Happiness for many days together"—then teasingly demanding—"Ask yourself my love whether you are not very cruel to have so entrammelled me, so destroyed my freedom"—and finally sensuously self-indulgent—"Will you confess this in the Letter you must write immediately and do all you can to console me in it—make it rich as a draught of poppies to intoxicate me—write the softest words and kiss them that I may at least touch my lips where yours have been." This is the tone that moved Matthew Arnold to declare that Keats lacked "character and self-control."

Arnold's judgment of Keats's self-control is truly applicable only to the later letters, written in the grip of fatal disease. Earlier, a healthy sense of reality tempers his passion: continuing the same first letter to Fanny, he writes, "But however selfish I may feel, I am sure that I could never act selfishly: as I told you a day or two before I left Hampstead, I will never return to London if my Fate does not turn up Pam or at least a Court-card." Following the progress of these letters from July 1819 to August 1820, when Keats appears to have written directly to Fanny for the last time, we see clearly that self-control diminishes as circumstances continue to gather like clouds above him. Again, Keats realistically foresaw this possibility in his character. "I doubt much," he admitted to Fanny (8 July 1819), "in case of the worst, whether I shall be philosopher enough to follow my own Lessons." There is no question that the later love letters of Keats are disturbingly self-indulgent and demanding; a healthier Keats would have scorned or laughed at them. Not many of us have to confront "the worst" as dramatically as he did.

We turn now to the poems. When Milnes wrote that in his biography he would leave "the memorials of Keats to tell their own tale," he did not mean the letters only. In fact, given his willingness to edit and omit parts of the letters for the sake of discretion, we may presume that he meant the poems first and the letters only as background and filler. As his authority he cited Wordsworth, who in his "Letter to a Friend of Robert Burns" upheld the right of authors to privacy. "Our business is with their books," Wordsworth had claimed, "to understand and enjoy them. And of poets more especially it is true,—that if their works be good, they contain within themselves all that is necessary to their being comprehended and relished."[10] Perhaps Wordsworth was feeling especially sensitive about Annette Vallon when he proposed this approach to biography, which succeeds in being at once Romantic (in its stress on the personality in the work) and discreet (in its willful neglect of the life beyond the work). Certainly no modern biographer would accept it; in effect, it renders biography as we know it otiose. The twentieth-century biographer accepts and evaluates all manner of evidence, and, especially after the Modernist period, when poets made a practice of hiding behind masks and distorted personae, he is likely to be much more wary than Wordsworth of that which appears autobiographical in a writer's creative work. Nonetheless, the poems of a writer like Keats may still be autobiographical to some extent, insofar as they present a self-portrait of the poet at the time he wrote them, as well as the concerns on his mind. The question, finally, is this: How much of our image of Keats comes straight from the poems?

The early poems of Keats are the most transparent, as might be expected. In virtually everything written before *Endymion*, which was his first great test, Keats is trying his wings, bravely announcing his hopes and candidly revealing his fears. Several generalizations are possible. First, the importance of friendship to Keats, which is obvious in the letters, is here confirmed. The poetic letters that he writes to George Felton Mathew, Charles Cowden Clarke, and his own brother George are certainly conventional, in keeping with the eighteenth-century genre of the verse epistle, but they are also clearly sincere efforts to reach out to this "brotherhood of song," to rejoice in the small community that shares his reverence for the "genius-loving heart."[11] Keats was not, as some later readers tried to make him, an isolated *poète maudit*.

Second, Keats's extraordinary absorption in literature is clear. He was not, by all reports, a bookish adolescent, and he did not have the classical education of, say, Coleridge or Shelley; yet his first known poems, written when he was around eighteen or nineteen demonstrate his literary inspiration by their titles alone: "Imitation of Spenser," "To Byron," "To Chatterton," "Ode to Apollo." They are weak, cliché-ridden pieces, but they introduce the young poet looking for a voice.

Concomitant with this fascination for the literary life is the natural desire to partake of it. Keats's trembling ambition to be "among the English Poets," most evident in the early poems, is the strongest motivating force in his life. It is poetry, he writes to Mathew, that brings "a feeling/ Of all that's high, and great, and good, and healing" (lines 9–10).

But Keats's ambition is not a simple matter, even in these apparently naive early verses. He was too conscious of his own obscure background, his sketchy education, and, above all, his as-yet undeveloped talent to proclaim his future greatness with an undivided heart. In what seems a reflex action, he invariably pulls back immediately after declaring his ambition, often using extravagant self-deprecation to veil his fear that he may not be worthy: "I am in doubt," he writes in the epistle to Mathew, "whether at all/ I shall again see Phoebus in the morning:/ Or flush'd Aurora in the roseate dawning!" (lines 20–22) In the epistle to George, he begins by wondering, in just the same vein, if he should ever hear Apollo's song. So passionately devoted is the young poet to his art that his greatest fear is that his ability may not equal his passion.

"Sleep and Poetry," the last, longest, and most ambitious poem in Keats's first volume, offers a résumé of all this early work and a kind of poetic itinerary. Again he declares his self-conscious hope:

> O poesy! for thee I hold my pen,
> That am not yet a glorious denizen
> Of thy wide heaven—

and then he goes on to foresee the path of his literary career:

> O for ten years, that I may overwhelm
> Myself in poesy; so I may do the deed
> That my own soul has to itself decreed.
> . . . .
> First the realm I'll pass
> Of Flora, and old Pan: sleep in the grass,
> Feed upon apples red, and strawberries,
> And choose each pleasure that my fancy sees.
> (lines 96–98, 101–4)

This is in fact an acurate description of Keats's early poetry, especially of *Endymion*, which would be his next major project. But he knows already that this kind of loosely mythological verse, full of "white-handed nymphs in shady places" (line 105), will not be enough for him as he matures:

> And can I ever bid these joys farewell?
> Yes, I must pass them for a nobler life,
> Where I may find the agonies, the strife
> Of human hearts.
> (lines 122–25)

Again, this is an accurate prediction, as far as it goes: Keats was indeed to become increasingly concerned with the human predicament, and with a tragic sense of loss, as almost all of his major later poetry shows. Posed against all the scholarly talk about Keats's "mentors"—Hunt, Haydon, Hazlitt—and the influence they had on him, the sharp self-awareness of "Sleep and Poetry" reveals an independent, strong-willed young poet, quite conscious of his own powers and ready to exercise them. But instead of the "ten years" that he modestly requested, he was to have just four.

Endymion, Keats's four-thousand-line "trial of invention," can be a quagmire for the biographer. In the story, a melancholy young shepherd, hungering for fame, falls hopelessly in love with a pale moon-goddess and pursues his ethereal desire through a profusion of incidents, finally resigning himself to the human love of an Indian Maid, who reveals herself as the moon-goddess in the last twenty-two lines. Is this legend autobiographical? Many critics have tried to sort out the parable, finding in it personal allegory.[12] Certainly, the young Keats longed for communion with an ideal beauty; almost as certainly, he was recognizing at the same time that it would be possible only by embracing the earthly, by achieving sympathy with the human. Beyond this point, the biographical critic's footing grows slippery, as we will see when we consider Amy Lowell's immense effort to elucidate the poem. For the student of Keats's life, the main fact of *Endymion*, as W. J. Bate explains, is the process of writing such a massive poem.[13] Having set himself a task, he simply had to accomplish it, no matter what the result. It was, he knew well, something to put behind him.

After completing that enormous project, which he recognized in its Preface as "a feverish attempt," Keats had to move on, and he indicates his new personal direction in several smaller, more penetrating poems. The problem with *Endymion* had been inherent in the proposal: it was too large, and he had too little to say. In his poem "On Seeing a Lock of Milton's Hair," written while he was revising *Endymion* for the press, Keats acknowledges this need for greater wisdom: "Pangs are in vain—until I grow high-rife/

With old philosophy" (lines 29–30). The next day, as he sat down to reread *King Lear*, turning to the great tragedy for renovation, he wrote a sonnet on the occasion, and scored the "golden-tongued Romance" of *Endymion* for its inadequacy:

> Leave melodizing on this wintry day,
> Shut up thine olden pages, and be mute.
> Adieu! for, once again, the fierce dispute
>   Betwixt damnation and impassion'd clay
>   Must I burn through; once more humbly assay
> The bitter-sweet of this Shaksperean fruit.
>   (lines 3–8)

There is almost a sense here that the poet must punish himself for having so indulged in the easy prettiness of *Endymion*; at the least, he must submit to a new trial, by tragic fire.

Three months later, a verse epistle to John Hamilton Reynolds ("Dear Reynolds, as last night I lay in bed") makes it clear that these concerns about greater knowledge are deepening. The poem, which was not intended for publication, begins lightly, with literary chat and references to common acquaintances; but it soon comes to a boil. Just as Keats had in the early epistles declared his poetic ambitions and then announced his modest doubt, here he wonders about his ability to resolve the questions that crowd into his mind:

>   to philosophize
> I dare not yet!—Oh never will the prize,
> High reason, and the lore of good and ill,
> Be my award. Things cannot to the will
> Be settled, but they tease us out of thought.
>   (lines 73–77)

This rough verse letter, addressed to his closest poetical friend, discloses the young poet's evolving thought about some of his most abiding preoccupations, anticipating the great odes of the next year. It is in these short, occasional pieces, rather than the larger, more polished efforts, that Keats is most closely autobiographical; here, more than in any of the poetry until the last tormented love poems to Fanny Brawne, his own hopes and fears come closest to the surface.

The great poetry of the last year of writing is more likely to tease the biographer out of thought. A large part of Keats's mature effort, after all, was to create a poetry that was less subjective, less like the moods of one's own mind. He had learned more, through both reading and experience, so that he was better able to sustain a narrative without falling back on references to his own situation. And, most important, his poetic talent had completely matured, enabling him to transfigure that experience in ways that make it extremely risky to claim that any particular passage is autobiographical. Robert Gittings, especially in his early studies, has indeed discovered many ingenious links between the poems and actual places, events, and readings in Keats's life; but his listing of apparent "real" sources for the creative work nearly suggests that Keats possessed no independent imagination.[14] Still, despite the poet's desire not to be self-absorbed in the later poems, he does reveal himself in some key passages.

Hyperion, that massive block of Grecian marble, was intended to be the opposite of the loose and episodic *Endymion*. But like *Endymion* it is first an exercise, an attempt at something Keats had never tried before. Paradoxically, it is the very absence of a personal voice in *Hyperion* that suggests something autobiographical. For Keats wrote the fragment while keeping watch over his consumptive brother's last days, when he was understandably troubled. The result, this austerely impersonal narrative, now seems one part Milton and one part self-control. As he wrote to Dilke at the time (21 September 1818), "I am obliged to write, and plunge into abstract images to ease myself of his countenance his voice and feebleness." The story of *Hyperion* recounts the fall of the Titans: it is a tale of loss. And, although Keats is careful not to take sides, it is hard not to hear his voice in the speech of Oceanus, explaining his response to calamity:

> to bear all naked truths,
> And to envisage circumstance, all calm,
> That is the top of sovereignty.
> (II, 203–5)

The great effort of *Hyperion* faltered soon after Tom's death. Perhaps Keats could not have sustained the Miltonic idiom anyway; perhaps he was unsure of his narrative. But it seems clear that one reason for turning to *The Eve of St. Agnes* was for relief from the severe majesty of *Hyperion* and its associations with Tom. Besides, this was a story of young love, and Keats himself was obviously fascinated by it, having met Fanny Brawne just several months earlier. The dangers of overzealous biographical reading of the poems have been amply illustrated by Gittings' analysis of *St. Agnes*, which suggests that Keats spent an amorous night with a friend named Isabella Jones just before writing the poem; J. Middleton Murry shows how extremely doubtful the sensational speculation is.[15] Still, it is not farfetched to see Keats's identification with the young lover, as he cheers his hero on ("Now prepare,/Young Porphyro, for gazing on that bed"). As he said to his friend Richard Woodhouse (letter of Woodhouse to John Taylor, 19

September 1819), he would "despise a man who would be such an eunuch in sentiment as to leave a maid, with that Character about her, in such a situation." Those who have questioned Keats's "manliness" or humor might reread these passages.

Beyond the general fascination with love, which is natural enough in an ardent young poet, biographical conclusions are difficult to draw from the poems that focus on relations between men and women. To say that "La Belle Dame Sans Merci" and *Lamia* demonstrate deep-seated ambiguities in Keats's own view of women is not to explain much, but it will have to suffice. There must be a limit to the reading of biography into poetry: where a poem stands clearly on its own as an autonomous world, without apparent reference to the poet's incidental life, the biographer should tread with caution. All kinds of conclusions have been extorted from the later poems of Keats, especially in regard to his relationship with Fanny Brawne; some of them will be evaluated in following chapters. But this is an area in which Wordsworth's focus on an author's works alone simply leaves the biographer short: Keats's small collection of great completed poems (including the odes and *Lamia*) may reveal the workings of his creative mind, but for recoverable facts about his earthbound life we must look elsewhere.

There is, though, one final fragment of special autobiographical interest: *The Fall of Hyperion*. It seems that Keats worked on this "Dream," which is essentially a new introduction for the fragment he abandoned early in 1819, in the summer and fall of that year—virtually until he stopped writing altogether. As incomplete and textually muddled as it may be, this new fragment shows both a striking change in style and remarkable consistency of personal stance. Apparently under the influence of Dante, Keats returns to a first-person narrative, recounting a dream in which he meets a "High Prophetess" who can tell him about salvation. In many ways the *Fall* is far more complex and compelling than any of Keats's early autobiographical works; and yet, it still displays his doubts about the poetic vocation, and in more penetrating—because more experienced—terms than ever before.

Early in this new vision, the poet turns to the "Holy Power" of his dream and exposes the same fears that Keats had revealed in those naive epistles four years before, as he was just starting out:

> "Majestic shadow, tell me: sure not all
> Those melodies sung into the world's ear
> Are useless: sure a poet is a sage;
> A humanist, physician to all men.
> That I am none I feel, as vultures feel
> They are no birds when eagles are abroad."
> (I, 187–92)

Here even the value of poetry is called in doubt: the use of "sure" in lines 187 and 189 is clearly the narrator's wishful attempt to convince himself of something he fears untrue. But the Shadow is maddeningly elusive, as a Shadow should be: she gives no answer to his first concern, about poetry in general; and to the vital question—what manner of man am I?—she answers with a question.

> "Art thou not of the dreamer tribe?
> The poet and the dreamer are distinct,
> Diverse, sheer opposite, antipodes.
> The one pours out a balm upon the world,
> The other vexes it."
> (I, 198–202)

Clearly, the questions have deepened in both real and symbolic significance since the first poems; the stakes have grown. But the doubts are essentially the same. That a poet who had in one year written a handful of the most perfect poems in the language should still be tormented by such doubts is remarkable, but characteristic of Keats, who could never let his devotion to a poetic ideal stand unchallenged. He enters and exits with the same questions.

This survey of the autobiographical content of Keats's works should provide both a sourcebook and a basis of comparison for the study of the biographies that followed. It may be helpful, before moving on, to stop and consider the character of the man depicted in these letters and poems. Although Keats never offers an extended self-portrait—in fact, he deliberately avoids what he might call "doting" on himself in a Wordsworthian mode—there emerges from his works a clear picture of a young man between the ages of twenty and twenty-five.

He was, above all, energetic, with a force that mixed equal parts of youthful ardor and literary ambition. This is the quality that moved Lionel Trilling to call Keats's letters heroic, and it is a primary reason that Keats continues to fascinate readers. He was never afraid to think in the largest terms of the endeavor before him, to "storm the main gate" of experience, in W. J. Bate's phrase about Samuel Johnson. "Why should we be owls, when we can be Eagles?" he wrote to Reynolds (3 February 1818). At the beginning of his career he was willing to leap "headlong into the Sea" in undertaking the great challenge of *Endymion* (to J. A. Hessey, 8 October 1818); near the end, disappointed and diseased, he still wrote about travelling to Italy "as a soldier marches up to a battery" (to Shelley, 16 August 1820), and, once arrived there, nervously settled into his "posthumous existence," he continued to summon up puns, "in a sort of desperation," to keep up Severn's and his own spirits (to Brown, 30 November 1820).

Keats's courage, as seen especially in the letters, was not abstract but clear-eyed and deeply practical, because his sense of reality, nursed by difficulties, was stern. "I would reject a petrarchal coronation," he wrote to Bailey (10 June 1818), "on accou[n]t of my dying day, and because women have Cancers." The addition of that last phrase is characteristic: Keats, who was later to watch his younger brother grow pale, and spectre-thin, and die, understood suffering. His attempt to comprehend the world as a "vale of Soul-making" (in the great journal letter to George and Georgiana Keats in the spring of 1819) constitutes an acceptance of the tragic life: "Do you not see how necessary a World of Pains and troubles is to school an Intelligence and make it a Soul?" And yet the realization does not harden into simple doctrine, declaring that even evil is for the best. Perhaps because Keats's mind was still young, thinking at random, he remained open to circumstances, and retained an awareness of realities that overwhelm philosophy. Soon after the drastic hemorrhage of February 1820, when he apparently offered to break the engagement with Fanny, he wrote sadly to her, "I would mention that there are impossibilities in the world."

Again, we should not allow the sombreness of that final year to darken our image of Keats as a social creature. Under the strain of financial and medical adversity, he was capable of writing that he hated the world (to Fanny Brawne, 25 July 1819), especially its fashionable society (to Georgiana, 15 January 1820). But the earlier poems and letters show that he was a "genial spirit," as George Bernard Shaw called him, and not "The Daintiest of Poets," as one Victorian reviewer declared.[16] Besides the fellow-feeling apparent in the verse epistles and letters to his siblings, Keats shows a positive gusto for company, especially in the heady winter of 1817–18, when his acquaintance with Haydon and Hunt led to parties involving Lamb, Wordsworth, Hazlitt, and other London lions. And although the natural inclination of his humor was not racy, like Byron's, he could write with relish of ribald puns and earthy talk, as, for instance, when he describes for his brothers (5 January 1818) the sexual wordplay at a recent dance. It is likely, considering his youth and modest stature (both social and physical), that Keats was politely reticent when he stepped into company. As the warmth of his correspondence with such older, more established figures as Hunt and Haydon shows, however, he readily won friends.

Notwithstanding a gift for camaraderie, Keats was not by nature a joiner; his preference for intimacy with his siblings and a small circle of friends is clear in the letters, where the same names recur frequently throughout the five-year span. Herein lies one of the reasons why biographers have been able to say little of substance about his politics and religion. Although he clearly inclined to the liberal view in politics (his literary career began in frank admiration of "Libertas" Hunt, and later, in financial straits, he considered writing periodical reviews for pay, "on the liberal side of the question"), he never gave much of his energy to a cause, unlike the other major Romantics. His indignation at the mistreatment of the poor is evident in *Isabella* and in several letters, but organized politics simply did not engage him; he was more interested in individual men and women, books and versification.

A man's religion is, of course, a harder nut to crack; but again, much of Keats's view appears to arise from a fierce insistence on individual integrity. As in politics, he began in the sphere of the skeptical Hunt and produced a sonnet, "Written in Disgust of Vulgar Superstition," composed with Huntian ease in fifteen minutes. Although it would be unfair to draw grand conclusions from this early effusion, the attitude announced in the title remains constant throughout most of Keats's career, until the darkness of the deathbed provoked new doubts. What troubled him most about the Church were "the pious frauds of religion," as he describes it in a letter to George and Georgiana (19 March 1819), especially the hypocrisy of clerics and outspoken believers. He thought his own "system of salvation," formulated in the letter on the "vale of Soul-making," superior to the Christian philosophy. But again the principal fact is that the institutions of religion, like those of politics, did not much interest Keats; for the most part, he rejected them as self-serving, and moved on to philosophical speculation of his own. As we shall see, Keats's religion, like his humor, was to prove especially problematic for nineteenth-century biographers, who could not fit him into the available poetic molds.

Given Keats's relative obscurity, it is not surprising that no full-length biography should have appeared for over twenty-five years after his death. But his former friends and associates, whose Keatsian connections have been chronicled by Hyder Edward Rollins, were not idle. Their efforts to establish his name, though fragmentary and largely unpublished for many years, form both the first chapter of Keats's biography and the documentary basis for most of the ensuing scholarly work.

The early history of Keatsian biography is a study in the literary infighting so typical of the Romantic period. During his life, it had seemed that the circle of Keats's friends, many of whom were acquainted through other, generally artistic, connections, was a fairly cohesive group of young men sharing many ideals. (A sharp exception is the enmity between Hunt and Haydon that started and grew as Keats watched helplessly.) But soon after his death, it became clear that the group had held just one thing in common: an admiration for Keats. Their shared affection, which could have been a rallying point, was in fact to become a wedge between bickering friends.

John Taylor, the dominant partner in the publishing house of Taylor and Hessey, which published Keats's last two volumes, was the first of the circle to propose a memoir. After all, he was in a sense the literary executor of the young poet, who had asked Taylor to distribute his books to friends after his death. But the announcement of the proposal that Taylor placed in the *Morning Chronicle* of 4 June 1821 seemed to show "indecorous haste" to Keats's friend Charles Armitage Brown, who questioned the bookseller's motives.[17] And Leigh Hunt, always spoiling for a literary scuffle, claimed that he would offer no aid unless Taylor submitted the memoir to Brown. Hunt seems to have suspected that John Hamilton Reynolds, who was planning a memoir of his own, would come off as the hero of friendship in Taylor's version. Charles Cowden Clarke, who had befriended Keats as a schoolboy at his father's school, was also reported to be compiling a memoir. In the midst of this tangle, John Taylor's proposed biography simply never materialized. He did manage to collar Keats's guardian for a remarkable interview that was to become an important part of the biographical record, but the project of a documented biography of Keats was dropped, not to be completed in that generation.[18]

The inability to gather letters and papers was not enough to stop Leigh Hunt, who included in his lively (if not always trustworthy) reminiscences entitled *Lord Byron and Some of His Contemporaries* (1828) the first memoir of Keats to see print. In fact, Hunt is responsible for the first two biographical notices of Keats, for he was surely the author of a very favorable sketch published the same year in John Gorton's *General Biographical Dictionary*.[19] In these two accounts, as always, Hunt championed his young friend; he presents Keats as a proud and sensitive but manly poet of great promise caught in a web of political animosity, disease, and heartache (although delicacy forbids the naming of Fanny Brawne). As he made no effort to compile documents, Hunt can hardly be called a biographer; but his evenhanded appreciation of Keats's poetry and personality helped establish the younger poet's name, and provided a firsthand account by someone who, satisfying one of Johnson's requirements for the biographer, had "eat and drunk and lived in social intercourse with him." Hunt's portrait was also indirectly responsible for the early appreciation of Keats in America: it was the basis for Cyrus Redding's sympathetic introductory memoir in the 1829 Galignani edition of *The Poetical Works of Coleridge, Shelley, and Keats*, which was published in Paris and sold not in England but in the United States.[20]

Naturally, Hunt's reminiscences did not please all of Keats's former friends. As we shall see, Charles Brown was especially disenchanted by Hunt's dwelling on Keats in sickness rather than in health. Moved by news of the Galignani edition in 1829, Brown finally started work on his own biography. The sketchy result, which remained unpublished until 1937, is disappointing. Brown's vision (which, as any reader of *Otho the Great*, the poetic drama he dictated to Keats, can attest, was never very penetrating) was especially clouded by two problems. First of all, he suspected George Keats of wronging his brother financially, and this suspicion created a rift that prevented Brown from obtaining documents from George and those who sided with him, including Reynolds and Dilke. Secondly, Brown was never able to distance himself emotionally from the controversies surrounding his friend. The manuscript that he compiled, which was delivered once as a lecture but never completed as a text, consists largely of invective against the unfeeling critics who had made a scapegoat of an innocent young poet for their own political purposes. Brown himself may have recognized the inadequacy of his memoir, for he made little effort to publish it before leaving England in 1841 to start a new life in New Zealand; instead, he left the manuscript to his chosen successor, Richard Monckton Milnes.

With the entrance of Milnes—an established figure of the next generation, a minor poet who had never known Keats and was therefore above the squabbles of his old friends—a new chapter of the story opens.

3

Strange Customs
Richard Monckton Milnes

It is almost the definition of a gentleman
to say he is one who never inflicts pain.
—John Henry Newman, *The Idea of a University*

The Life, Letters, and Literary Remains of John Keats that Richard Monckton Milnes published in 1848 is not a masterpiece of biography. Diffident in its aims, slight in analysis, and lackadaisical about facts, it cannot compare to the more artful or compendious work of biographers like Southey, Moore, and Lockhart. Nonetheless, the first full-scale biography of Keats did achieve its primary goal: to establish and advance the fame of the poet. The story of Milnes's effort to gather sources and adapt them to his own use—to reconcile the accounts of Keats's quarreling friends, rectify the exaggerations of a Romantic legend, and satisfy both public and personal standards of dignity—is virtually an exemplum of mid-nineteenth-century biography.

The selection of Richard Monckton Milnes as the first biographer of Keats was in several ways a natural one. Although he had never met his subject (Milnes was just twelve years old when Keats died), he was a literary man well acquainted with the Romantic era, a minor poet himself. As a member of the Apostles at Cambridge, he had shared his friend Tennyson's early admiration for Keats. Charles Brown, upon entrusting the biographical material to him in 1841, wondered if Milnes's higher status and affluence would allow him a sympathetic understanding of Keats's struggle for recognition and worldly security.[1] As it happens, Milnes had first turned to the poetry of Keats and Shelley as an antidote to the lordly *ennui* of Byron, and he found Keats's social obscurity rather an attraction than otherwise.[2]

In fact, Milnes is best remembered as an usher of unknown talent into the world. As Henry Adams recalls in the best brief portrait of him, "Milnes was always unearthing new coins and trying to give them currency."[3] The most dazzling of his new coins was the young Swinburne, whose eccentric demeanor and brilliant talk constituted a vivid part of the American private secretary's education. Some readers have found in Milnes himself the same kind of eccentricity: Mario Praz describes a "Mephistophelean malice" that corrupted Swinburne and hosted strange parties at a sinister home in Yorkshire.[4] It is true that his remarkable library included an extensive collection of erotica and the writings of Sade, and that he sometimes enjoyed a parlor game of *épater le bourgeois*. But the portrait that arises from the remarks of his acquaintances is that of a kind, gruff, portly fellow who never quite found his calling. He lacked the political acumen and commitment to justify his membership in Parliament; he realized, to his credit, that he was not a poet of the first rank, even though Landor once placed him there; and, although he had charm, he failed to win the hand of his one true love, who later found her own calling. (In retrospect, he does seem an unlikely husband for Florence Nightingale. Years later he gracefully commented, "If she had [married me] there would have been a heroine the less in the world and not a hero the more."[5]) Monckton Milnes may have been, as Disraeli found him (and caricatured him in *Tancred* as Mr. Vavasour), vain, trivial, sometimes "smutty"; but he was not diabolical. It is oddly fitting that this extravagant dillettante who was called "the Bird of Paradox" should be remembered above all for his most disinterested act, *The Life of Keats*.

When Milnes accepted the project from Charles Brown in 1841, he inherited not only Brown's sketchy "Life" but also the personal animus of Keats's old friend. Upon sending Milnes his memoir (19 March 1841), Brown insisted that any publication retain two of his prominent reasons for writing: first, an attack on the *Quarterley Review* and *Blackwood's Magazine* for their critical abuse of Keats; and second, a correction of Leigh Hunt's emphasis on the poet's pathetic illness. The requests are understandable, coming from an associate who wished to set right what he considered a mistaken image. But the result was not entirely happy. Whereas Milnes's distance from the controversies of Keats's life promised an ideal biographical position of objectivity, Brown's stipulations threatened to compromise that stance. To be sure, the new biographer had a remarkable opportunity to step forward independently when both Brown and George Keats, Brown's imagined nemesis, died soon after the consignment of the papers. Whatever one might say about Milnes's eccentricities, however, he lived by a code of gentlemanly honor, and he intended to honor his commitment to Keats's friend.

In truth, Charles Brown had a more powerful means of control over the first biography of Keats: his "Life," as incomplete as it might be, remained Milnes's most important source. Hyder Edward Rollins's *The Keats Circle* records the results of Milnes's desultory efforts to collect other materials. Cowden Clarke sent a memoir of the school days, Joseph Severn anecdotes from Italy; nearly all of the old associates contributed letters to or from Keats, except for William Haslam, who had misplaced his, and Leigh Hunt, who, perhaps testy about this proposal to supersede his own portrait of Keats, wrote that he had already published his statement.[6] All told, the biographer's effort to gather information was dilatory and only partially successful. But it should be remembered that he had to do more than run half over London for some of his facts: Severn was helpful but still in Italy; Bailey was so inaccessible (in Ceylon) as to be presumed dead; and several of Keats's most important letters were languishing in Kentucky, available only in highly unreliable transcripts. In effect, Milnes faced the modern biographer's problems of distance and inaccessibility of sources without the benefit of modern transport or electronic tools. And the fact that several of the sources were personally at odds made his effort to reconcile and synthesize all the more difficult. Among the many associates of Keats who proposed their own memoirs or promised help to the eventual biographer, only Charles Brown finally collocated his memories with the available papers. To appreciate Milnes's endeavor we must understand the resources and abilities of the man who entrusted it to him.

Brown's manuscript resources were invaluable. His "Life" is the primary source for eight of Keats's letters, and he provided more than three quarters of the unpublished "remains" in Milnes's first edition. This is not to say that the writing of his friend's life came easily to him, or that he was the ideal biographer. His practical, bookkeeper's mentality had pleased Keats especially for its "disinterested character" during their friendship; later, however, he was unable to gain sufficient perspective for the writing of a clear account. He explained to Leigh Hunt (21 December 1836) that painful memories had made him defer the project for so long, and he admitted to Milnes (29 March 1841) that "there is no cool judgment in me while I am reading any thing by Keats."

Such emotional attachment made Brown hypersensitive to any criticism of his late friend. One of his excuses for the long delay of the memoir was that he wanted to wait until Keats's fame had risen; otherwise, he feared, any effort to describe the poet's genius might provoke the critics to a fresh outburst of mockery (thus he advised Severn against erecting a Hampstead monument to Keats in a letter of 7 February 1823). This concern may have been justified, for the partisan viciousness of contemporary reviewers knew no bounds; but Brown failed to appreciate the paradox that the very memoir that he kept deferring was a potential means of redeeming Keats's name.

Brown's extreme caution, combined with procrastination and an excess of sentiment, simply made him a poor remembrancer. Before the publication of *Lord Byron and Some of His Contemporaries*, he warned his friend Hunt that "the living are rarely satisfied" (20 February 1827); afterwards he proved his point by complaining about what was actually a complimentary treatment of him in the book, concluding, "I hate the present literary fashion of being personal" (14 September 1829). This is not the credo of a born biographer.

Nonetheless, Brown's "Life of John Keats" has real value beyond its importance as a source book for Milnes: it also marks the beginning of a crucial correction of the general image of the poet, a correction that was not to attain public acceptance until well into the next century. His task, quite simply, was to alter a conception of Keats that had been set in print by three formidable contemporaries: Shelley, Byron, and Hunt. Shelley's stirring tribute in *Adonais* portrayed the dead poet as "a pale flower by some sad maiden cherished," cut before blooming. Then Byron, who, without reading deeply in Keats, reacted violently to the Huntian cavilling against Pope in "Sleep and Poetry," published in *Don Juan* the famous faintly-praising lines about the talented but pathetic young poet who was "snuffed out by an article." Last, and most important to Brown, was Hunt's brief essay on Keats in the 1828 book on Byron.

Although Keats had not always approved of Hunt's jaunty manner and chaotic family, the older man was ever a generous champion of his onetime protégé, and the portrait in *Lord Byron* is frankly laudatory, including well-chosen quotations of Keats's best work. Hunt even recalls telling Byron before the publication of *Don Juan* that the story about Keats's death by criticism was apocryphal, but notes caustically that the noble poet just wouldn't give up "a joke and a rhyme together."[7]

Still, Charles Brown was right to see Hunt's account as one of the barriers to a true understanding of Keats. One problem, as Brown realized, was Hunt's estimate of their young friend's illness. In the very first paragraph of the essay, Hunt describes three points that find no confirmation in any other memoir on Keats: that he was prone to tears upon hearing of noble deeds, because of "ill health"; that he would hold out his own hand and dramatically call it "the hand of a man of fifty"; and that he was a seven-months' child (I, 408). We know that Keats was occasionally given to emotional or even morbid exaggeration; Hunt may well have heard and seen such things. But his account offers no context for them, and his emphasis on Keats's infirmity colors the entire profile, revealing his own taste for melodrama. His critique of *Endymion*, for instance, excuses Keats's "poetical effeminacy" "by reason of his ill health" (I, 419). Later, quoting the "Ode to a Nightingale," Hunt sentimentalizes by stating that Keats composed it "while he lay sleepless and suffering under the illness which he felt to be mortal" (I, 435). The notion of an all-pervasive illness that casts a fatally Romantic pall over Keats's entire career is, of course, simply wrong. He wrote *Endymion* during a healthy summer at least two years before the onset of disease; while he may have contracted tuberculosis from his brother Tom before the spring of the great odes, it had certainly not yet reached an active phase.[8] Finally, although Hunt denies Byron's witticism about the killing critique (Hunt was glad to criticize Byron for anything), he does little to dismiss the idea that the critics brought on Keats's demise. Feeling responsible for the abuse that the younger poet received simply because of association with his own notorious "Cockney" group, Hunt apologizes for not noticing that "an injury . . . was done to a young and sensitive nature" (I, 425). "A delicate organization," he continues, "which already anticipated a premature death, made him feel his ambition thwarted by these fellows" (I, 426). Hunt can be excused for his sensitivity on this point, and even for his misunderstanding of the illness: Keats had deliberately had little contact with his old friend between the time when he was writing *Endymion* in the summer of 1817 and the period after the first hemorrhage made disease undeniable, when, alone and desperately ill, he once again moved in with the Hunts in the summer of 1820. Disillusioned by the quarrel between Hunt and Haydon, and hoping to avoid further guilt by association with the Cockneys, Keats had kept his distance. Hunt's distorted conclusions in *Lord Byron* are understandable. Given the final image of his sick and tormented friend, he naturally magnified the importance of the illness, and (looking back nostalgically as he wrote eight years later) extended its duration over a period about which he knew relatively little. Charles Brown, contemplating his own memoir, recognized that "every sentence" of Hunt's account was intended to raise Keats's honor and fame; "but what does that matter," he wrote to Dilke (17 December 1829), "when he manages to make him a whining, puling boy?" In this regard, at least, Brown was percipient, even prescient: the image of the whining boy was one that later biographers would especially have to combat.

Unfortunately, Brown's effort to correct the Romantic image of a feeble, wounded Keats was largely thwarted by another part of his program, which Milnes was to inherit. No matter what he might say about the poet's forthright and stouthearted constitution, his extensive castigation of partisan critics provides ammunition for doubters. Throughout the "Life" he vents his indignation against the "accumulation of ridicule and scoffs" against Keats's character, which "did worse than tear food from the mouth of a starving wretch, for it tore honour from the poet's brow."[9] We can hardly help wondering, with Lord Byron, how such a "fiery particle" as Brown's tough-minded Keats could be so ruinously sensitive to criticism. It appears that Brown, personally stung by the fierceness of the reviews, simply wanted to have it both ways. As the modern editors of his "Life" explain, "Had Charles Brown been less a champion, he would have been more a biographer."[10]

It is likely, considering the bitterness that touched nearly all of the former friends who wanted to preserve their own views of the poet's career, that Brown was interested in defending not only Keats but himself. Possibly feeling guilty about not having accompanied Keats to Italy, Brown never wanted to concede that his friend was already mortally ill when he left England. Instead, he maintained that the disease was mental, tormented by an impossible love and exacerbated by hireling critics.[11] Again, the result was that the resolute masculine poet Brown admired became something closer to the brain-sick, critically wounded victim he deplored in the versions of Shelley, Byron, and Hunt. The legend was just too attractive to deny.

By the time Richard Monckton Milnes got around to publishing the book that he made out of Charles Brown's project, John Keats had been dead for twenty-seven years and the reign of Victoria underway for more than a decade. It is at least as difficult to characterize "Victorian biography" as it is to define its Romantic counterpart: six decades of rapid development, action and reaction are impossible to pigeonhole. But certain writers of the early twentieth century thought they knew most definitely what Victorian biography was, and they were just as sure that they didn't like it. Virginia Woolf was horrified: "Victorian biography," she wrote, "was a particoloured, hybrid, monstrous birth."[12] And her outspoken colleague Lytton Strachey was simply disgusted: he derided the "two fat volumes" that typically comprised Victorian biographies with "their slipshod style, their tone of tedious panegyric, their lamentable lack of selection, of detachment, of design."[13] Of course, a modern biographer like Strachey, who sought to define (and to justify) his endeavor by opposition to his predecessors, had an executioner's axe to grind. But many of his objections had some basis in fact, as we may see in considering what an early Victorian biographer like Milnes made out of the Romantic legend that he inherited from Charles Brown.

Milnes begins by following the practice of Moore and Lockhart: proposing to allow Keats to speak in his own words, he prefers "to act simply as editor of the Life which was, as it were, already written" (I, xix). In this regard Milnes, like his Romantic predecessors, used the "Mason method," which had been institutionalized by Boswell. Departing from this common intention, though, Milnes diverges from Moore and Lockhart in both method and motive. They had both thrown up their hands at the sheer mass of primary material available, and decided to publish as much as possible; so doing, they could hope to forestall critics who might find their accounts colored by close acquaintance with their subjects. As we shall see, Milnes had rather too little documentary evidence than too much, and he was far enough removed from Keats not to fear attacks on his objectivity. Yet, even more than the biographies of Byron and Scott, his *Life of Keats* is, as he admits, rather a "compilation" than a "composition" (I, vi).

One reason for the lack of analytical commentary in Milnes's biography is an essential diffidence: like Lockhart—but with more reason, as he knew so much less of Keats than Lockhart knew of Scott—he is reluctant to probe into the inevitably speculative realm of his subject's innermost concerns. And he buttresses this modesty, as we have seen, with the support of Wordsworth's "Letter to a Friend of Robert Burns," which maintains, in brief, that the private lives of authors are nobody's business. Rejecting the "Boswellian plan," Milnes's focus on the author's works alone seems an anticipation of the New Criticism, applied to biography. But such an anachronism involves a paradox, of course: the New Criticism, in an extreme reading, would not allow biography into the study of literature at all. As soon as Milnes starts equating life and letters, claiming that a poet's biography "can be little better than a comment on his Poems" (I, 2), he risks the Romantic extreme of reading the poetry as the life set to verse. Samuel Johnson had signaled the danger of a biographical interpretation of creative work nearly a century before, in his "Life of Thomson":

> The biographer of Thomson has remarked that an author's life is best read in his works: his observation was not well-timed. Savage, who lived much with Thomson, once told me how he heard a lady remarking that she could gather from his works three parts of his character, that he was a "great lover, a great swimmer, and rigorously abstinent"; but, said Savage, he knows not any love but that of the sex; he was perhaps never in cold water in his life; and he indulges himself in all the luxury that comes within his reach.[14]

Although the intellectual outlines of a poet's life may be, in Virginia Woolf's phrase, "written large in his works," the biographer, armed with knowledge from other sources, must not neglect the fine print.

Another problem with the decision to allow "the memorials of Keats to tell their own tale" was the obverse of the predicament facing Moore and Lockhart—a scarcity of materials. Although Milnes had managed, by means of his poetic reputation and his impartial position, to gather many documents from all parts of the Keats circle, he still had less than a quarter of the Keats letters now available. Without substantial narrative links, this scanty record is not sufficient for the subject to "tell his own story."

A practical reason for Milnes's editorial policy becomes apparent when we check the accuracy of his facts. He seems to have made little effort to verify details, and where he rests upon assumptions on the word of other accounts, he is often wrong. He commits, for instance, such large (and easily verifiable) errors as asserting that George Keats was older than John (the elder by fifteen months) and noting that Benjamin Bailey had died "soon after Keats." (Bailey was dismayed to read of his own death.) Less obvious, but more annoying in their cumulative effect, are many errors of personal detail (Keats's eyes were brown, not blue), chronology (letters are often cited out of sequence), and identification (the "Charmian" of a letter was understandably mysterious, but Milnes could have known that it was not the unnamed Fanny Brawne had he pursued of few available clues). Given this evidence of shaky factual foundations, it is no wonder that the biographer preferred to let Keats speak for himself.

In the process, Milnes made a choice that most early twentieth-century biographers would regret: he foreswore the biographer's claim to artistry. His two volumes are not particulary fat (in Strachey's terms) only because the materials from Keats's brief life were not abundant; even so they certainly lack selection and design. Nearly seventy per cent of the text consists of letters excerpted or *in toto*, gathered loosely in chronological sheaves. Strachey would have approved instead of a biography like Carlyle's *Life of Sterling*, which, disclosing far less primary material, is sternly shaped by the author's intention to compose something like a heroic poem. In comparison, Milnes's achievement, although stylistically competent and valuable as a documentary source, is both pedestrian and inconclusive. Not every biographer need climb on Carlyle's rhetorical rollercoaster in order to reach the goal of a vivid portrait, but we do hope for more informed commentary than his friend Milnes was willing to offer.

Of course, we should be wary of judging the first life of Keats in twentieth-century terms. Like many mid-Victorian biographers, Monckton Milnes proposed only to gather pertinent materials; for the purposes of many late twentieth-century readers, his compilation is more useful than the livelier but less reliable portraits provided by biographical artists like Strachey. Unfortunately, Milnes was not entirely true to his announced intentions: for a variety of reasons, he did not always allow his subject to speak for himself. Milnes's editing of his primary material brings us to a question crucial to Victorian biography—for that matter, to biography in general—the question of discretion. How much should a biographer tell, and how should it be told?

It is certainly not just to consider this dilemma the exclusive property of the Victorians. We have already seen how, at the height of the Romantic period, Southey maintained the honor of Lord Nelson with some discreet sleight-of-hand. And the question is still alive: as recently as 1966 another book about a dead hero prompted furious objections from many who believed that current practices should be as respectfully careful as Southey's.[15] But we are concerned here with general trends, and it is fair to say that the tendency of Milnes's time was toward more careful discrimination between what was done privately and what was accepted publicly. In his study of nineteenth-century biography, A. O. J. Cockshut concludes that the height of biographical reticence coincided roughly with the first half of Victoria's reign, from about 1840 to about 1875.[16] Near the beginning of this period, Lockhart records an 1820 discussion of the novelist Aphra Behn, whose books had been widely read sixty years before, even aloud; now Walter Scott's grand-aunt can't get through one, because of its "Charles II" manners. Scott understands, speaking of the "gradual improvement of the national taste and delicacy."[17] That gradual improvement, which endangered candor in biography, was to continue through much of the century.

We have already seen that one manifestation of increasing gentility in the practice of biography was the rejection of Boswell, or at least of Boswell's indecorous methods. The refusal of writers like Lockhart and Moore to "Boswellize" may represent an implicit recognition of their failure to equal him, but it also shows a basic resistance to the practice of painting a Flemish portrait of a man in all states of dress and undress. Probably more important—certainly more repugnant—to these nineteenth-century biographers were the memoirists whom they identified as working in the Boswellian tradition, even when the characterization was inaccurate. *The Life of Johnson* could be allowed as a *lusus naturae*, redeemed by the moral majesty of its subject. But when a controversialist like Leigh Hunt, who had already been jailed for libel of the Prince Regent, applied Boswell's techniques of (apparently) full disclosure and dramatically preserved conversation to his frankly critical account of Lord Byron—about whom there was much to be reticent—associates of the late poet cried foul. Thomas Moore, whose biography would appear two years after *Lord Byron and Some of His Contemporaries*, immediately responded with satiric vitriol:

> Next week will be published (as "Lives" are the rage)
>   The whole Reminiscences, wondrous and strange,

> Of a small puppy-dog that lived once in the cage
>   Of the late noble lion at Exeter 'Change.
> . . . .
> How that animal eats, how he moves, how he drinks,
>   Is all noted down by this Boswell so small;
> And 'tis plain, from each sentence, the puppy-dog thinks
>   That the lion was no such great things after all.
> . . . .
> 'Tis, indeed, as good fun as a Cynic could ask,
>   To see how this Cockney-bred setter of rabbits
> Takes gravely the Lord of the Forest to task,
>   And judges of lions by puppy-dog habits.[18]

One Boswell had been enough.

But the growing caution in biography of the first half of the nineteenth century was not just a sign of increasing bourgeois gentility, or of reaction against less decorous practices initiated by Boswell; it was also, as Richard Altick suggests, a reflection of profound needs in the English consciousness of the time.[19] The vast popularity of the many biographies of Nelson indicated a demand for national heroes; Shelley's "Defence of Poetry," written in 1820 but not published until 1840, presented the Poet as a cultural hero; and in that same year Carlyle dedicated two of his six lectures on "Heroes and Hero Worship" to the literary man as a seer, providing impassioned theoretical support for Shelley's visionary poetics. The new emphasis on individual, poetic heroism was, in large part, a protest against the advance of an industrial society, where Mammon reigned. Of course, the protest could also lead in another direction: before the end of the century rugged individualists like Samuel Smiles were outlining the heroic way to serve Mammon, in biographies of Carlyle's Captains of Industry.

As the century progressed the need for human heroes became increasingly clear. With the impact of the new geology and, later, of evolutionary biology, educated Victorians saw evidence that the Sea of Faith was receding, and a new humanism presented itself as a way to fill the frightening gap. Auguste Comte's positivism proposed a religion of humanity, complete with a list of 538 heroes and benefactors of mankind—a new saints' calendar.[20] In the very year that Milnes published his *Life of Keats*, the Pre-Raphaelite Brotherhood was compiling a "list of immortals," which placed Keats at the same level of immortality as Homer, Dante, and Alfred the Great.[21] Given the public desire for reassurance, it would hardly do for niggling biographers to demonstrate that any of their heroes had feet of clay.

Richard Monckton Milnes, at any rate, would not do so. First of all, his subject's heroism had yet to be ascertained. The recondite tastes of the Pre-Raphaelite Brotherhood not being a reliable gauge of public opinion, Milnes had to spread the fame of his obscure young poet. Keats's origin was one of the first matters he had to establish—or disestablish, in this case, as his aim was to refute a small part of the legend. Charles Brown, probably remembering that the critics had cruelly made much of Keats's "Cockney" associations, had objected to Hunt's statement that Keats's "origin was of the humblest description" (*Lord Byron*, I, 409). "As the world goes," Brown wrote to Dilke (17 December 1829), "such bald and untrue words may have a bad effect,—for they are untrue, as far as *humblest* is concerned; . . . he, Hunt, ought to have known better, because, though it is true a God was born in a manger, his admirers, or worshipers, or priests would rather he had been born in a palace." The "humblest" of origins may have appealed to "Libertas" Hunt, but Brown was afraid that the fascination for "natural," underprivileged poets like Burns had passed. In his own "Life" of Keats he wrote simply that "John Keats was born in Moorfields on 29th October 1796. His father was a native of Devonshire, and married a daughter of the proprietor of an inn."[22] Milnes, in turn, corrected the year of birth to 1795, and expanded the account so far as to explain that Keats's father was employed by the proprietor of the inn, whose main concern was a livery stable.

As usual, Milnes leaves the reader to judge the facts, although he does add that Keats's father was entirely free from "any vulgarity or assumption on account of his prosperous alliance" (I,4). Naturally, his presentation of the facts reveals his inclinations. James Russell Lowell, who later wrote his own summary account of Keats's life, took Milnes to task for trying to make his subject "a gentleman by brevet":

> We shall not be too greatly shocked by knowing that the father of Keats . . . "was employed in the establishment of Mr. Jennings, the proprietor of large livery-stables on the Pavement in Moorfields, nearly opposite the entrance into Finsbury Circus." So that, after all, it was not so bad; for, first, Mr. Jennings was a *proprietor*; second, he was the proprietor of an *establishment*; third, he was the proprietor of a *large* establishment; and fourth, this large establishment was *nearly* opposite Finsbury Circus,—a name which vaguely dilates the imagination with all sorts of potential grandeurs.[23]

Lowell's stridently democratic sarcasm is not fair to Milnes's slight distortions, but it does suggest the way that style may heighten—or, later, in Strachey's hands, reduce—the mere facts. Later, in the abridged "memoir" prefixed to editions of Keats's *Poetical Works*, Milnes omits all mention of the father, saying only that Keats was born "in the upper rank of the middle class"[24]—at best an exaggeration. One other subtle touch colors Milnes's account of Keats's social status. At the beginning of his preface, he records his meeting with Charles Brown, "at the villa of my distinguished friend Mr. Landor, on the beautiful hill-side of Fiesole" (I, ix). This opening may be more a piece of name-dropping than anything else, but it has the disingenuous effect of casting an exotic, aristocratic glow over the life of Keats. Milnes's apparent desire to heighten Keats's status seems inconsistent with the fact that he himself was partly attracted by the poet's humble origins. But perhaps it was, as William Michael Rossetti sternly judged, "a concession to that deadly spirit of flunkeyism in the British people which, after doing its pitiful best to embitter Keats's life on the score of his unexalted origin . . . is still capable of wishing to suppose that he was more like a member of 'the upper rank of the middle class' than what he really was—a member of a very middling rank in the middle class."[25] More likely, Milnes simply misjudged the new reading public, which was actually thrilling to tales of obscure heroes like those of Dickens; he seems to have thought that in order to carry on Brown's battle against class-conscious critics he had to prove that Keats was not a Cockney.

But the care taken to present the subject's origins properly would be wasted should the poet then go on to express himself like a Cockney. Given the primacy that Milnes accords to Keats's own words in the narrative, it seems odd to late twentieth-century readers that he should then feel free to alter the letters. As the critic Diane Johnson says, this practice is "a bit like copying out a passage of somebody else's work in your own hand before submitting it to hand-writing analysis."[26] As we saw in Lockhart's re-creations of Scott's correspondence, however, it was common practice at the time. William Mason, desirous of maintaining Gray's scholarly reputation, had corrected his "don't" to "do not," his "oaf" to "simpleton," his "brag" to "boast." Later in the nineteenth century, J. W. Cross preserved his image of the high-minded George Eliot by editing all colloquialisms and humor out of his late wife's letters.[27] Thomas Moore shows himself an even more radical revisionist in a letter to John Murray on the composition of his *Byron*:

> I am getting on very well, having satisfied myself with respect to the Italian Loves, by omitting the whole of the letter about Angelica (making a love the less) and transferring the long account of Mar-

garita from the place of its date (where it jars with our Guiccioli Romance) to an earlier period where it chimes in with his dissolute course of life, and thus keeps the character of each epoch more consistently.[28]

Milnes's editorial infidelities are never so drastic (Keats could hardly have afforded a love the less), but nonetheless he silently manipulates his text. His editing provokes several important questions about biography. Of the material he omits, how much is attributable to an early Victorian ethos of reticence, intended to preserve dignity? How much is concealment amounting to falsification? How much is simple unawareness of what has been omitted? Milnes's omissions and alterations are so extensive that a thorough treatment of them would require an entire dissertation; even Harold E. Briggs's 800-page annotated edition of the biography (unpublished doctoral dissertation, University of Minnesota, 1943) occasionally summarizes the changes rather than cataloguing them. A brief survey of Milnes's practice may reveal much about the controversial issues in Keats's life, the standards of midcentury biography, and, of course, about the biographer himself.

Perhaps the most obvious example of Milnes's manipulation of Keats's letters is his deletion of disparaging words about living or recently deceased associates. Of course, this practice was common. Samuel Johnson had identified the problem when he considered writing his "Life of Addison": "As the process of these narratives is now bringing me among my contemporaries I begin to feel myself 'walking upon ashes under which the fire is not extinguished,' and coming to the time of which it will be proper rather to say 'nothing that is false, than all that is true.' "[29] Although Keats had been dead for twenty-seven years when Milnes published in 1848, many of his associates and loved ones still survived, and the liveliness of the letters they exchanged concerning him, now preserved in *The Keats Circle*, proves that the embers were still warm. It is not surprising, then, that Milnes should omit names and entire sentences from Keats's letters. In two letters to Benjamin Bailey, for example (8 October 1817 and 23 January 1818), Milnes leaves blank the names of Reynolds, Hunt, and Haydon when Keats describes their "retorting and recriminating" over petty matters. At another point (the letter to Reynolds on 21 September 1817) he omits phrases on Hunt's tendency to dominate conversation, and an objection to the company of Mrs. Hunt. Later, Milnes deletes an unflattering comment on the man who was Poet Laureate when the biography was published: "I am sorry," wrote Keats to his brothers (21 February 1818), "that Wordsworth has left a bad impression wherever he visited in Town—by his egotism, Vanity and bigotry." Milnes may have had England's strict libel laws in mind when he excised such passages; within the next decade Elizabeth Gaskell would be forced to soften some judgments in her *Charlotte Brontë* (1857) when threatened by legal action.[30] It is more likely, though, that Milnes's own sense of propriety dictated the omissions. When there was some chance of wounding those still alive, he reasoned, silence is the best policy.

The most notable silence in the first biography of Keats is the total omission of the name and circumstances of Fanny Brawne. To the regret of Charles Brown, Leigh Hunt had broken the ice on Keats's romantic life by mentioning "a very tender circumstance" in *Lord Byron and Some of His Contemporaries*. Without naming the beloved, Hunt had described a sentimental scene in which the teary-eyed Keats, weakened and embittered by illness, announced that "his heart was breaking" (p. 440). Brown, writing to Miss Brawne for help on his own memoir (17 December 1829), seems at first to sound the modern note of honest disclosure: "As his love for you formed so great a part of him, we may be doing him an injustice in being silent on it." Then the pragmatist intervenes. "Indeed something must be said especially as Hunt has said something." And finally he explains the sad necessity of discretion, in a timid lament of *O tempora! O mores!*

> We live among strange customs; for had you been husband and wife, though but for an hour, every one would have thought himself at liberty to speak of, and all about you; but as you were only so in your hearts, it seems, as it were, improper.

Thus Milnes's chief source, while recognizing the desirability of fuller portraiture, passed on a sketch that essentially omitted the poet's grand passion. And other potential sources, like Severn or Charles Dilke, either knew little or thought little of Fanny Brawne.

Monckton Milnes also upheld these "strange customs." But his explanation did not go so far as Brown's in suggesting that the requirement for open examination of the young lovers was a validating marriage. For him it sufficed that the matter was private and recent:

> Where personal feelings of so profound a character are concerned [he wrote], it does not become the biographer, in any case, to do more than indicate their effect on the life of his hero, and where the memoir so nearly approaches the times of its subject that the persons in question, or, at any rate, their near relations, may be still alive, it will at once be felt how indecorous would be any conjectural analysis of such sentiments, or, indeed, any more intrusive record of them than is absolutely necessary for the comprehension of the real man. (I, 242–43)

"The true gentleman," as Newman was soon to describe him, "guards against unseasonable allusions, or topics which may irritate."[31] It was not, as Brown had suggested, merely a question of containing each emotion within the proper legitimatizing institution, such as marriage. Rather, in Milnes's more extreme—and more typical—view, private emotion itself was not the proper province of the biographer. Significantly, where Brown had omitted the name of Fanny Brawne in the declaration "I like xxxxxxxx and I cannot help it" (23 September 1819), Milnes omits the whole sentence. "Thus, in compiling the life of a poet," wrote a reviewer in *Blackwood's*, "we maintain that a literary executor has purely a literary function to perform." "Whatever refers solely to domestic existence is private, and ought to be held sacred."[32]

The trouble with Milnes's approach was, as Charles Brown had realized, that he could not describe the "real man" in Keats without some analysis of the love that so preoccupied the poet during the final two years. But he tried. In order to maintain some fidelity to the facts without violating sacred privacy, Milnes briefly alludes to Keats's romantic attachment without naming names, making of it another piece of the legend. Here was an obscure young surgeon's apprentice of exquisite sensibility, suffering not only from financial need and critical abuse but also from a pathetic *grand amour*. This "one intense affection," which cannot be identified, would "hasten, by its very violence, the calamitous extinction against which it struggled in vain" (I, 173). The biographer does his best within the limitations that he accepts: unable to draw a real portrait without mentioning his subject's romantic passion, unwilling to publish facts about it, he describes it in the most general of terms, leaving his readers to ponder what G. Wilson Knight has called "the evidence of asterisks."

Another problematic area revealed by Milnes's editing of the letters is the matter of Keats's religion. Here again, as in the treatment of Fanny Brawne, he was certainly constrained by the wishes and the feelings of surviving associates. As we have seen, Keats's questioning spirit doubted the worth of institutionalized faith. After his death, friends who were already sensitive to the scoffs at his reputation took care not to spread another source of provocation to critics. When Milnes was preparing the *Life*, Severn wrote from Italy that the pious Haslam was "most anxious that no passage relative to poor Keats's despair about Religion should be published"; Severn himself, whose anguished letters describing Keats's last days in Rome frequently mention that very despair, twice encouraged Milnes to edit out any material he found troubling.[33]

Given this combination of exhortation and license from friends of the late poet, Milnes could hardly publish the manifest evidence of Keats's doubt. Among the many irreligious notes that he omits are passages involving skepticism (for instance, a lament on the "pious frauds of Religion"), irreverence (an oath taken "by the delicate toenails of the Virgin"), and anticlericalism (several remarks on hypocritical parsons). Following Severn's advice, the biographer completely dismantled his final letters from Rome, removing the companion's agonized admissions that Keats had "no religion to support him," that he was suffering horribly, and that several times he longed for the release of suicide.

Although modern readers may regret that any such deletions were made in the scanty record of Keats's thought, we can understand how the pressures of propriety and living friends made some suppression of apparent blasphemy necessary, at least until the poet's reputation might be established. But Milnes's extreme measures indicate that he was especially sensitive on the subject. After the death of Tom Keats, for example, John wrote to George and Georgiana (16 December 1818) in a characteristically tentative tone, "I have scarce a doubt of immortality of some nature or other." Rather than leave well enough alone, Milnes takes the opportunity to suggest that Keats was in his own way a true believer, changing the statement to "I have a firm belief in immortality" (I, 246). As we will see, the difficult question of Keats's religion continued to stymie biographers throughout the nineteenth century, partly because of distortions and evasions like these.

But Milnes's evasions in the *Life of Keats* are not limited to the suppression of sensitive matters like romance and religion, where the publication of an improper gesture or opinion could embarrass or wound a surviving associate. Indeed, it appears that once he started altering Keats's letters, he found that nothing short of wholesale revision would do, down to the very texture of the poet's language. A brief exploration of Milnes's modifications of his text may best reveal his biographical policy and practice. In the process, we may learn just what Keats meant to his first biographer.

It must be remembered, first of all, that Monckton Milnes did not undertake the biography in the way that most scholars would proceed today. Busy as he was with politics, society, and his own poetry, he simply did not take pains to ascertain his texts or verify his facts. We know that his younger friend Coventry Patmore served as an amanuensis, making transcripts of certain letters for use in the biography. But we do not know how many letters he copied, or how much editorial independence he had. One of the transcriptions now in the Keats Collection of the Houghton Library at Harvard, for instance, omits a bawdy passage from a letter by Keats to his brothers (5 January 1818), in which the young poet describes "getting initiated into a little Cant." Milnes also omits the passage in the *Life*, leading us to wonder to what extent the author of *The Angel in the House* dictated the tone of Keats's letters in the final version, for the changes and errors are many. A copy of Volume I that belonged to Edward Moxon, the publisher of the biography, shows how negligent Milnes apparently was: Moxon collated and corrected thirty-four of the letters, and found more than two hundred errors in approximately one hundred and fifteen pages of text.[34] We may never know exactly what circumstances caused such inaccuracy; but we must hold the biographer responsible.

Many of the changes in Milnes's text of Keats's letters represent either slips of the pen or attempts to clarify what was hurried or murky in the original. But even some of these alterations are suspicious. For instance, Keats wrote in a typically hasty way to Haydon (10 May 1817), "When, Tom who meets with some of Pope's Homer in Plutarch's Lives reads some of those to me they seem like Mice to mine." Milnes's version not only cleans up the wandering syntax—for which the common reader may thank him—but changes the sentiment: "When my brother reads some of Pope's Homer, or Plutarch's Lives, they seem like music to mine" (I, 37). Perhaps the alteration arose from a misreading of Keats's hand, which is usually quite clear; if so, it is a convenient error for a biographer who would rather present a modest, struggling young poet than a scorner of English classics.

Naturally, Milnes regularized the often sloppy spelling and syntax of Keats's letters, which was common practice at the time. Anyone who has looked into Rollins's authoritative edition of the letters knows that the poet's spelling was often dreadful (the devoted Keatsian might say "unrefined"), his punctuation at best erratic ("spontaneous"). Milnes's Keats, however, is a proper grammarian, although nowhere is it announced that the text has been altered. The only loss here, even to the most dedicated Keatsian, is the sense of a young mind hurrying from thought to thought, reckless of errors.

Somewhat more serious is the "regularization" of his vocabulary. As we might expect, Keats's letters show that he enjoyed playing with language, recording moods with a wide range of tones. Even in a sober or gloomy moment he will turn a verbal trick, sometimes to mask a deeper concern, sometimes to raise his own spirits, sometimes because he simply can't resist a bad pun or a twisted quotation. But such inconsequentiality seems to have troubled Milnes. Although his own wit was sharp (he once mocked his corpulence by observing, "My exit will be the result of too many entrées"), he apparently subscribed to a public view of the poet that anticipates Matthew Arnold's requirement of "high seriousness." Thus, when Keats descends into a nonsensical aside or a deliberate Cockneyism, Milnes usually excises it. In the "Negative Capability" letter, for example (21, 27 December 1817), Keats writes playfully about Shelley, "I think he has his quota of good qualities, in sooth la!!" and Milnes omits the final three words. Describing recent quarrels among close friends (to George and

Tom, 13 January 1818), Keats injects some levity by quoting *Humphrey Clinker*, "Lawk! Molly there's been such doings," and the biographer deletes the quotation. Similarly, Milnes's alterations of unusual coinages appear to be motivated more by aversion for a loose or Huntian style than by a need for clarity. He changes Keats's occasional use of "feel" as a substantive ("how comfortable a feel it is") to more standard forms ("how comfortable it is to feel"), and Keats's expressive adjective "spleenical" becomes the proper "splenetic."

But Milnes's concern for the language in Keats's letters goes beyond proper usage, to propriety in the social sense. He would not publish Keats's occasional ribaldries, whether they were half-serious or entirely in jest. When Keats tries to cover his anxiety about financial affairs by using a jaunty metaphor in a letter asking his publishers for special consideration (10 June 1817), Milnes omits the opening sentence: "I must endeavor to lose my Maidenhead with respect to money Matters as soon as possible." When Keats laments the miseries of Robert Burns in a letter to Reynolds (13 July 1818, dated 11 July by Milnes), regretting that Burns "talked with Bitches—he drank with Blackguards," the biographer corrects him again: "He talked, he drank with blackguards." And when he teases James Rice (24 March 1818) about the "little Barmaids" he has recently met ("One asked whether you preserved a secret she gave you on the nail"), Milnes simply chooses to cut the entire passage.

In fact, the editing of the letters in the first *Life of Keats* shows Milnes to have been especially sensitive about sexual matters. Considering the unbuttoned atmosphere of the Regency, the correspondence contains relatively few remarks on the subject; the biography makes public almost none at all. From an early letter to Reynolds, for instance, in which Keats describes customs on the Isle of Wight (17 April 1817), Milnes deletes one of the conclusions: "I must in honesty however confess that I did not feel very sorry at the idea of the Women being a little profligate." Whenever there is some suggestion that Keats may have been more experienced than the biographer would care (or be able) to explain, the suggestion is removed. For example, Keats wrote to Bailey (30 October 1817), "When I am not suffering for vicious beastlinesss I am the greater part of the week in spirits"; to Tom (26 July 1818), "With respect to Women I think I shall be able to conquer my passions hereafter better than I have yet done." In all likelihood, both sentences are innocent of the meanings that Milnes probably feared (the first being an exaggerated reference to drinking and the second to a passionate imagination), but he took no chances, excising them both. (In the 1867 edition Milnes seems to have noticed something that he missed in 1848. The first edition prints in its entirety a letter to Bailey [8 October 1817] that includes the offhand remark, "The little mercury I have taken has corrected the poison and improved my health." By 1867 Milnes apparently realized—as William Michael Rossetti was to suggest twenty years after—that mercury was commonly taken for syphilis, among other things. At any rate, he removed the words "corrected the poison and.")

One more matter that was later to trouble biographers of Keats is conspicuously absent from Milnes's version of the correspondence. That is his drinking, and indulgence in social life in general. The winter of 1817–18, when Keats was just being introduced to the company of London literati, was undoubtedly the liveliest social period of his life, and several letters to his brothers record both the exuberance (the passage on "a little Cant") and the fatigue ("suffering for vicious beastliness") involved. The Houghton Library holds transcripts of these letters by Patmore, including the following examples of high spirits: "I pitched upon another bottle of claret-port"; "I astonished Kingston at supper with a pertinacity in favour of drinking, keeping my two glasses going in a knowing way"; "we played from 4 till 10." And on the first page of the transcripts stands the biographer's *non imprimatur*: "These letters I did not print. R. M. M." Because of this policy, from a later letter (to George and Georgiana, 14 February–3 May 1819) he would have to delete the word in brackets here: "I never drink [now] above three glasses of wine." If Milnes had been more candid about Keats's moderate drinking, perhaps Haydon's later claims about the poet's dissipation (published in 1853) would have made less of a stir among mid-Victorian critics.

Of course, it would be possible to explain all of these omissions by the same principle that silenced Keats's irreligion: publication of such improprieties would wound surviving intimates of the poet. This concern was doubtless a part of the biographer's motivation, but there seems to be something deeper. Why, we may ask today, was Monckton Milnes so eager to erase the existence of minor flaws—language that was ungrammatical, slangy, or racy, the vaguest hints of sexual experience, decidedly small-time drinking —that would hardly trouble a modern biographer? We may be tempted by a quick and easy answer: he was, after all, a Victorian. Surely much of Milnes's editorial policy must be attributed to his own reading of current standards of decency; as suggested above, the mid-nineteenth century was especially sensitive about the private conduct of its heroes. There is, though, more to Milnes's practice than a desire to conform to a public standard that was at best extremely elusive. As with most serious biographies, the biographer's heart had its reasons that the public reason could not know.

Even the most general reading of the psychology of biographer and subject will suggest that Milnes was moved to write his only biography by more than aesthetic appreciation of Keats's poetry. The author of *Endymion* was already known—insofar as he was known at all—through the legend perpetuated by the commentary of Shelley, Byron, Hunt, and Brown. Milnes summarizes the charges brought against him: he was "a wayward, erratic, genius, self-indulgent in conceits . . . weak, gluttonous of sensual excitement, querulous of severe judgment, fantastical in its tastes, and lackadaisical in its sentiments" (I, xvi–xvii). Clearly, this figure is not a hero for Victorian or any other readers; if the biography was worth writing, the image would have to be refuted. But if we subtract the word "genius" from that description of Keats, the words might also bring an indictment against the private side of Richard Monckton Milnes. We need not subject him to psychoanalysis (difficult, of course, at this late date) to know that beneath the gruff exterior there lay an essentially effeminate character that took forbidden pleasure in various kinds of sensual excitement. "The thing I was intended for by Nature is a German woman," he wrote half-seriously to a friend, "I think Goethe would have fallen in love with me."[35] And we need not repeat Mario Praz's description of satanism to surmise that such a public figure was, at the least, uneasy about his unacceptable private habits.

It is not surprising, then, that Milnes should come to the defense of an admired poet who had been accused of similar weaknesses. In response, his most emphatic term of appreciation is a word that was to become heavily freighted in later Victorian discussions of literature, and especially of Keats—the word "manly." Dismissing hints of loose conduct, Milnes insists that Keats led a "plain, manly, practical life" (I, 74). The poet may have been fascinated by pagan beauty, but "he kept his affections high and pure above these sensuous influences" (I, 24). Even the self-indulgent lushness of his early verse is clearly explicable by noble aims: he was led astray by an admirable allegiance to uneven models like Leigh Hunt and Spenser (I, 10), whom he soon outgrew.

There is useful truth in Milnes's portrait, but it is also clear that he protests too much. Of course, his emphasis on "manliness"—a compound of self-reliance, earnestness, and clean, simple living—is an exaggeration meant to counterbalance the established legend. In order to maintain it, though, he feels obliged to ignore contradictory evidence, often by erasing it from the record. A manly Keats would not stoop to Cockney slang, or loose talk about women, or indulgence in "claret feasts." Moreover, Milnes also adjusts the physical image of the poet to his own ends. He describes Keats reciting the "Ode to a Nightingale" to Haydon in "his deep grave voice" (I, 245), whereas Haydon mentions only a "tremulous undertone," and Bailey remembers a "sweet-toned voice, 'an excellent thing' in *man*, as well as 'in woman'."[36] Again, Milnes suggests that Keats's protruding lower lip gave his face a pugnacious look, but all other accounts (and most pictures) agree that the upper lip was actually more prominent. These are small details, and they may represent mistakes rather than willful distortions. Still, it appears likely that Milnes, in an attempt to portray the most masculine Keats possible, was too ready to misinterpret the evidence in favor of his own design.

We may now deplore deliberate inaccuracies like those that mar the first life of Keats. But at the same time we should recognize that Monckton Milnes's standard of decency was not just self-defense, wish-fulfillment, or submission to convention—although all of these come into play. It was a felt ethos, in which manliness was only part of a larger ideal of gentlemanliness. If Milnes himself could not entirely live up to it—and who could?—at least he could use it to protect a hero whom he found essentially true to its aims. Although his customs of evasion and omission may seem strange to us, they seemed to him necessary for the preservation of the hero's dignity. If he had been more forthright and thorough, some of the problems discussed in the following pages might not have arisen. But if he had not undertaken the difficult task at all, Keats's reputation would doubtless have grown far more slowly, documents from surviving friends would probably have been forgotten or misplaced, and our loss would be the greater.

4
Inheriting Unfulfilled Renown
Mid-Victorian Estimates

Ah! Wherefore all this wormy circumstance?
—*Isabella*

In his ground-breaking study of Keats's influence on the later nineteenth century, George Ford asserts that "in the reputation of no other English poet has the question of personality played such a significant role in its development."[1] Not surprisingly, the personal imprint is deepest during the period between the publication of Milnes's first edition of the *Life and Letters* and the next spate of biographical work, when Sidney Colvin and William Michael Rossetti published new studies of the life. Ford demonstrates the extent of Keats's more purely literary influence by adumbrating the echoes of Keatsian lines and methods that seeped into the poetry of several Victorian writers, sometimes—as in the case of Matthew Arnold— against their will. To a greater degree than even Ford allows, biography conditioned the rise of Keats's reputation. In the thirty-nine year hiatus between the *Life and Letters* and Colvin's *Keats* (1887), critical views of Keats's temperament, his illness, and his love for Fanny Brawne almost always qualified a just evaluation of the poetry, and sometimes overwhelmed it. This "dry period" in Keats biography (by far the longest period in which no new memoir appeared) actually presents a fertile study in the subterranean development of a biographical image.

The primary reason for the long gap between biographies of Keats is that Milnes (who became Lord Houghton in 1863) ruled the field. The *Life and Letters* was generally recognized as the definitive work, and no new study was likely to appear as long as Fanny Brawne survived (she died in 1865) and Milnes held the Keats material he had gathered. Meanwhile, several new editions of the poetry were published, in close to fifty separate issues, reflecting the rise of Keats's literary stock.[2] Milnes himself, apparently cheered by the reception of the biography, continued to publish. In 1856 he printed a separate edition of the *Poetical Works*, with a thirty-seven page memoir that resuscitates Benjamin Bailey but otherwise repeats the factual errors of 1848. In 1867 a new edition of the *Life* appeared. By now Lord Houghton was able to add material—a memoir by Severn, information from Haydon's *Autobiography*, the cancelled first preface to *Endymion*, which was unavailable in 1848—and to name some names of figures now deceased, such as Reynolds and Haydon "retorting and recriminating" in the letter of 23 January 1818. But the "one profound passion" of Keats's life remained nameless, as the memory of Fanny Brawne was still fresh. Moreover a chance for refinement of the poetical canon was missed. In 1857 Milnes had printed for private circulation the previously unpublished version of *Hyperion* that is now known as *The Fall of Hyperion*; unfortunately he always considered it a first draft (even though Charles Brown's memoir clearly spoke of the "remodeling" of *Hyperion* into a "Vision"), and thus neglected the poetic evidence that Keats was still sternly questioning the value of poetry at the end of his career.

Finally, in 1876 Lord Houghton presented the Aldine edition of the *Poetical Works* of Keats, with a new memoir that named Fanny Brawne for the first time, eleven years after her death. He had apparently made little effort, however, to ascertain her identity, for he introduces her as "a Miss Brawn, a lady of East-Indian parentage,"[3] perpetuating his mistaken reading of Keats's letters to George and Georgiana (October 1818) that describes a cousin of Reynolds as a "Charmian." (Harry Buxton Forman corrected this error soon enough, in the introduction to his 1878 edition of the letters of Keats to Fanny Brawne.) Nonetheless, we must give Houghton credit for understanding—and for stating, finally—the essential tenor of Keats's love. First, "during the autumn and early winter of 1819 Keats was under the silent influences that almost made up his existence—his imperfect health and his passion for Miss Brawn" (p. xxv); later, in 1820: "During this sad year his relations with Miss Brawn were his constant thought and occupation, and left him in an alternation of 'happy misery or miserable misery' " (p. xxviii). There is no evidence that the long-withheld naming of Fanny Brawne caused any stir among readers in 1876. With this edition, Richard Monckton Milnes completed his long and valuable service to Keats and Keatsians.

Although the period between Milnes's first edition and the new lives of 1887 saw little fresh biographical analysis, an image of John Keats was gradually developing, as though in a photographic darkroom. Rather, many images were developing: any life will present at least as many versions as it has observers. By focusing on several important observers of Keats in mid- to late-Victorian England, we may trace the extrabiographical life of a poet's image (the life found outside formal biographies), in order to understand the transformed materials of the next biographers.

It might be said that Keats brought the Pre-Raphaelite Brotherhood together, both literally and figuratively. In May of 1848, Dante Gabriel Rossetti admired a newly exhibited painting of "The Eve of Saint Agnes" by William Holman Hunt, and introduced himself to the painter. Soon the two were deeply involved in the eccentric but influential group—all of them Keatsians—that, transmuted by the various talents of Rossetti, Millais, Burne-Jones, Morris, Swinburne, and others, made an enormous impact on late nineteenth-century art and taste. The early members were delighted, in the autumn of 1848, to see Milnes's generous biography confirm their enthusiastic "discovery" of the little-known poet, especially when they read a letter of Keats to George and Georgiana (31 December 1818) praising pictures of a literally pre-Raphaelite fresco from the Campo Santo at Pisa. The vigorous charm of Keats's character in the letters must have counted as well. "He seems to have been a glorious fellow," Rossetti effused in a letter to his brother.[4] That image would not always shine so innocently; by the end of Rossetti's often painful journey, it was to take on a sombre glow.

As has often been noted, the Pre-Raphaelites admired Keats especially for his pictorial power, his use of color, his interest in medieval literature, and his sensitivity to the supernatural. His best work—for them, this meant "La Belle Dame Sans Merci," *The Eve of Saint Agnes*, and the curiously stylized fragment "The Eve of Saint Mark"—embodied an exotic intensity that freed them from both eighteenth-century convention and nineteenth-century vulgarity. Dante Gabriel Rossetti, in his early enthusiasm, typified their response: he called Keats "the one true heir of Shakespeare,"[5] anticipating Matthew Arnold's famous judgment of Keats's Shakespearean qualities. That the major poems showed little interest in social matters was of no importance to Rossetti, who seldom sought explicit political commentary in art. (For William Michael Rossetti, whose 1887 biography of Keats I will treat in the following chapter, this "gap" in Keats's outlook was more troublesome; but he could never sway his older brother to his own strong preference for Shelley.) Rather, Dante Gabriel foreshadows the Aesthetes of the end of the century in seeing Keats's untrammeled artistic intensity as a basic virtue: "No pulpit," he wrote, "would have held Keats's wings."[6]

In fact, Rossetti's developing view of Keats's character prefigures the *fin-de-siècle* image of the poet in several ways. When the love letters to Fanny Brawne were published, sending a *frisson* of fascinated distaste through most Victorian readers, including staunch Keatsians, Rossetti was at first "greatly pained";[7] but he was never disgusted, and he soon made Keats's romantic torment a part of his favorable image. As the author of poems condemned for sensuality and the doomed lover of Elizabeth Siddal and Jane Burden Morris, he must have experienced the sense of persecution that is evident in a few of Keats's anguished letters; as a devotee of beauty who, having "lost on both sides" of painting and poetry, never accomplished his heart's desire in art, he clutched the fraternal example of the suffering artist to his bosom. Although Keats in his essential Englishness was far from the French *symbolistes* who popularized the image, his tragic career seemed to offer a paradigm of the *poète maudit*.

One manifestation of this sentimental (and, in cases like Rossetti's, at times self-pitying) icon is the annexation of the Keats story to the legend of Chatterton.[8] Shelley had been the first to draw the inevitable parallel, invoking Chatterton in *Adonais* (stanza XLV) as one of the other "inheritors of unfulfilled renown." Milnes, attempting to disarm criticism of his as-yet unproven hero, had extended the comparison: "That these Poems should be the productions of a young surgeon's apprentice, with no more opportunities of study and reflection than belonged to the general middle class of his time and country, is in itself a psychological wonder, only to be paralleled by the phenomenon of Chatterton."[9] But these observations, poignant as they are, focus on what Milnes calls "the unaccomplished promise of this wonderful boy" (reminding us of Wordsworth's "marvellous Boy" in "Resolution and Independence"), rather than on the painful death of the outcast. Keats himself had seemed to offer sanction for the comparison by writing a sympathetic sonnet on Chatterton in 1815 (first printed by Milnes in 1848) and by dedicating *Endymion* to the eighteenth-century poet. Again, though, the motives were not purely sentimental. Although Keats was doubtless drawn by the pathos of this "child of sorrow," he also genuinely admired the "purity" of Chatterton's language, finding it more "entirely northern" than the Gallic Chaucer or the Latinate Milton, and he patterned his own theory of "melody" in verse, according to Bailey, after the chiming vowels of lines like Chatterton's "Come with acorn cup & thorn."[10]

Thus what had been a Romantic interest in original genius cut short was becoming a Victorian sentimental legend, as Rossetti's later references to Keats and Chatterton demonstrate. In a series of late sonnets, Rossetti created a virtual pantheon of Romantic (or pre-Romantic) poets whose brave lamps of vision had been pathetically snuffed out. First is Chatterton, the model, whose "wild heart" could find no peace in English society, and who "craved a dart" from Death, to lie obscure in a "grave unknown." The rest ring variations on the theme: the visionary Blake, who took "for daily bread the martyr's stone"; Coleridge, whose "deepening pain" allowed him artistic power for only "six years, from sixty saved"; Keats, wandering in a Blakean London, "weary with labor spurned and love found vain"; and Shelley, whose literal and figurative boat had been engulfed " 'mid mists impenetrable" by "man's deed of hell."[11] Clearly, Rossetti not only pities and praises but also identifies with these martyrs of English song. Indeed, the composite portrait's psychological lineaments may resemble those of its author more than the features of any one of the subjects. This is an artistic re-creation of biography, following a model made after the writer's own image. Of course, we should not expect a sonnet to be factually exact. But we should recognize the effect it may have in fostering a popular image—especially when one of the next biographers is the sonneteer's admiring brother. Dante Gabriel Rossetti considered Chatterton "an absolute and untarnished hero"; examining some portraits of him, he remarked, "There is a savour of Keats in them."[12]

As every commentator of the period noted, the pathos of Keats's life and work was rooted in critical disfavor, unfulfilled love, and the blight of untimely illness. But the greatest of these was illness. Milnes had satisfied most readers that Keats was not snuffed out by an article.[13] Before the publication of the letters to Fanny Brawne in 1878, too little was known of the relationship for it to occasion much commentary. But, even though Milnes had edited the most graphic details out of Severn's letters, the pity of Keats's tubercular "decline" (as the disease was sometimes euphemistically called) was lost on no one.

Indeed, illness heightened the image of the *poète maudit* that was developing in the minds of subjective readers like Rossetti. As Susan Sontag explains in her suggestive study of *Illness as Metaphor*, tuberculosis is the Romantic malady *par excellence*.[14] In contrast to the steady, insidious attrition of the twentieth-century disease, cancer, tuberculosis manifests itself spasmodically, in the passionate extremes of febrile activity and desperate resignation, in the dramatic coughing of life's blood. It highlights and spiritualizes, refining the gross body. Although the tuberculosis bacillus can attack anywhere, the most common locus of attachment (as in Keats's case) is the lungs, and "a disease of the lungs is, metaphorically, a disease of the soul."[15] Such suffering was considered especially appropriate, of course, for those who lived by poetic inspiration. Shelley, in a lighthearted attempt to console Keats, wrote (27 July 1820), "This consumption is a disease particularly fond of people who write such good verses as you have done."

For "consumption," as tuberculosis was popularly known, was an "artistic" disease that created a new model for sensitive, languorous looks and fashionable martyrdom. "When I was young," wrote Gautier, "I could not have accepted as a lyrical poet anyone weighing more than ninety-nine pounds."¹⁶ Good health—which Keats the orphan and walker of hospitals valued long before his own declined—was simply banal. "I look pale," declared Byron, "I should like to die of a consumption." Why? asked Moore, who was himself tubercular. "Because the ladies would all say, 'Look at that poor Byron, how interesting he looks in dying.' "¹⁷ Of course, Byron was pushing pins into an absurdly inflated fashion. But he was to get his wish for an interesting disease, and his dramatic death added a heroic glow to his own biography. Many nineteenth-century writers seemed bent on proving that Goethe's opposition of the "sickly" Romantic to the healthy Classical was not merely figurative.

Furthermore (and this is especially instructive in the case of Keats), the passionate symptoms of tuberculosis were commonly taken as evidence of a fire burning within the victim, who was "consumed" by ardor.¹⁸ This diagnosis applies not only to the successful lover but also to those who repress their true sexual nature. "He who desires but acts not," notes Blake in one of his shrewdest aphorisms, "breeds pestilence." Keats himself seems to have subscribed to this theory, at least in the final months of agony, separated by disease from Fanny Brawne. "My dear Brown," he wrote from Naples (1 November 1820), "I should have had her when I was in health, and I should have remained well." Surprisingly, Milnes printed this passage in 1848 (without naming "her," of course), probably because he did not read it in a sexual sense. The implication that Keats's own passion generated the fatal disease suggests a tendency to self-destruction that was central to the image of the *poète maudit*.

Before the onset of the final illness, which became active in the dramatic hemorrhage of February 1820, Keats was decidely not the tubercular "type." Although unusually short (slightly over five feet in a time when five feet six inches was a good height), he was broad-shouldered, robust, and noted for pugnacity rather than languor. But it is the pathos of promise cut off by tragic illness, as narrated in the letters of Keats and Severn from Italy, that inevitably transfixes the reader's (and the biographer's) attention, distorting the general image through a trick of perspective. Milnes had often emphasized the genial spirits and "manliness" of his subject, but he could not resist the melodrama of the sickroom. Here is a description, adapted from Haydon's journal, of a visit to the ailing poet: "The very colouring of the scene struck forcibly on the painter's imagination; the white curtains, the white sheets, the white shirt, and the white skin of his friend, all contrasted with the bright hectic flush on his cheek and heightened the sinister effect: he went away hardly hoping."¹⁹ This passage is one of the few dramatically conceived scenes in Milnes's biography; it is the equivalent of Severn's deathbed sketch of Keats, with a crucial touch of color added. The death-blanched pall of the room vividly sets off the passionate disease burning within, which becomes an emblem of the tragedy of a poet dying young. Readers like George Gilfillan elaborated the metaphor, seeing in it a terrible beauty: "His genius lay in his body like sunfire in a dewdrop, at once beautifying and burning it up."[20] It is not far from this image to the "pang-dowered poet" of Rossetti's sonnet—the poet whose very gift, his ability to suffer eloquently amidst the numbing monotony of a sheet-white world, is his downfall.

It would be unjust to suggest that Monckton Milnes was entirely responsible for fostering an image of the pathetic young poet: he had stressed the pugnacious Keats who withstood unfeeling critical attacks, and, after all, Byron, Shelley, and Hunt had already popularized the portrait of the hypersensitive plant. A creative reader like Rossetti will often reach a conclusion that meets his own needs, even though it be a step or two from truth. But Milnes also offered support for misreading, in an occasional flourish of rhetoric. Although his manly Keats had not succumbed to viperous critics, the biographer still digresses to castigate the reviewers for political partisanship, and closes his story with a quotation from Shelley, about Byron: "And therefore men

>Are cradled into poetry by wrong:
>They learn in suffering what they teach in song."[21]

It is unfortunate that this conclusion should be so far removed from the main features of the portrait drawn in the biography, for it is but a step from Milnes's final note to the sentimental corollary that Keats's life was in a sense "perfect" after all. Shelley had hinted at such a view in the Neoplatonism of *Adonais*, where death, however painful it may be, is only an awakening from "the dream of life."

>From the contagion of the world's slow stain
>He is secure; and now can never mourn
>A heart grown cold, a head grown grey in vain.

Rossetti adapted this traditional elegiac consolation to his aesthetic concerns, fearing the effect of the modern world on any maturing poet: "Keats hardly died so much too early," he wrote in a letter of 1879, "not at all if there had been any danger of his taking to the modern habit eventually—treating material as a product, and shooting it all out as it comes."[22] Francis Thompson entertained the notion that Keats's life ended with poetic appropriateness in "The Cloud's Swan Song," claiming that he "died in perfect time,/ In pre-decease of his just-sickening song." These readers essentially wanted to freeze Keats in the attitude that Leigh Hunt had named for him—"the Young Poet," forever loving and forever fair. They interpreted the consumptive disease as a necessary conclusion to such an intensely creative life. "The talent itself," explained Matthew Arnold in a comparison of Keats to Maurice de Guérin, "is deeply influenced by their mysterious malady; the temperament is *devouring*; it uses vital power too hard and too fast, paying the penalty in long hours of unutterable exhaustion and in premature death."[23] There is no doubt about Keats's intensity—it was, after all, one of his artistic ideals, modelled on Hazlitt's "gusto"—an intensity that at times surfaced in passionate jealousy or morbid fears. In fact, Keats's last doctors followed a belief akin to Arnold's in forbidding the writing of poetry, for fear that it would excite him unduly and further devour his wasted body. But only an overemphasis on the pathetic final year allows the Victorian reader to make of Keats a *poète maudit*, forgetting the vitally healthy man who wrote almost all the poetry. Any reading that considers the life perfect and the final illness fitting, even self-generated, is neglecting the extraordinary vigor of Keats's often-stated desire to live and to achieve a fame that he saw eluding him.

If Dante Gabriel Rossetti was relatively untroubled by the publication of Keats's letters to Fanny Brawne in 1878, he was virtually alone in his unconcern. Those thirty-seven letters provoked loud dismay among Victorian readers, and they still test the equanimity of modern biographers. In the editor's preface, Harry Buxton Forman wrote that Monckton Milnes's reticence about Fanny Brawne was "proper enough, no doubt, thirty years ago, but surely now a needless affliction."[24] The reviewer from *The Athenaeum* (apparently Charles Wentworth Dilke, grandson of Keats's friend, who had founded the prestigious journal in 1828) begged to differ: "In life's battle an English gentleman would as soon think of picking the pocket of a dead comrade as of making public his love-letters."[25] Forman explained that his edition portrayed Keats's love "as perfectly as possible . . . without the revelation of things too sacred for even the most reverent and worshipful gaze"; James Russell Lowell responded in the margin of his copy (now in the Houghton Library at Harvard), "*What* in God's name *is* too sacred nowadays?" Although most readers have since agreed with Forman that Keats's love letters, however painful, are necessary "for our better knowledge of his heart," as recently as 1963 W. H. Auden was still affirming that they should never have been published.[26] My purpose here, however, is not to discuss the propriety of the publication of private letters, but to analyze their influence on the reputation of a writer, and especially on his biographical image. The outspoken opinions of such widely divergent representative men as Algernon Charles Swinburne and Matthew Arnold probably reveal more about their speakers than about their subjects, but they also suggest the enormous importance of biographical information in late-Victorian estimations of literature.

As a close associate of the Pre-Raphaelites and one of the "discoveries" of Monckton Milnes, Swinburne was naturally exposed to the phenomenon of Keats early in his career. At first, he approved. In an essay on Blake written between 1862 and 1865, Swinburne alludes briefly but unequivocally to the life, comparing "a man so perfect as Keats" to "a man so imperfect as Burns."[27] And in a review of Arnold's *New Poems* (1867), he lauds the poetry, noting that Keats was far more gifted than the French writer Arnold had compared him with, Maurice de Guérin. Swinburne considered editing a small volume of Keats for Moxon, along the lines of the edition he made of Byron, and did assist William Michael Rossetti in the selection of poems for Rossetti's 1870 text.[28] In his early enthusiasm, he also paid Keats the ultimate compliment of imitation, composing his own version of *Hyperion* in 1859 or 1860. But Swinburne's poetic debt to Keats is not extensive. Like William Michael Rossetti, he regretted the absence of the prophetic strain in Keats; and he eventually moved away from the Pre-Raphaelites in his preference for musical cadences over Keatsian pictorial richness.[29]

Swinburne's divergence from the influence of Keats was not, however, purely aesthetic: it was also powerfully propelled by the appearance of the letters to Fanny Brawne. His revulsion at Forman's little book found its way into verse published in 1884, reminding us of Tennyson's angry poem "On Reading a Life and Letters." But the voice of the four sonnets entitled "In Sepulcretis" (originally "Post Mortem") is distinctly Swinburnean:

> Make bare the poor dead secrets of his heart,
>   Strip the stark-naked soul, that all may peer,
>   Spy, smirk, sniff, snap, snort, snivel, snarl, and sneer:
> Let none so sad, let none so sacred part
>   Lie still for pity, rest unstirred for shame,
>   But all be scanned of all men. This is fame.[30]

Like Tennyson, who virtually edited his own biography by dictating strictly to his son what could be published and insisting that the rest be destroyed, Swinburne, who burned many of his own letters, was sensitive about privacy.[31] For an inscription to the sonnets he quotes Heine: "To publish even one line of an author which he himself has not intended for the public at large—especially letters which are addressed to private persons—is to commit a despicable act of felony." And, although he never names Keats, he identifies the object of his wrath as "*foreman* of the flock whose concourse greets/ Men's ears with bray more dissonant than brass" (emphasis mine).

The imagery of the sonnets is revealing. Swinburne describes the purveyor of the letters as an accomplice to voyeurs, whose curiosity is distinctly sexual:

> No rest, no reverence now: dull fools undress
> Death's holiest shrine, life's veriest nakedness.
>
> Strip the stark-naked soul, that all may peer . . .
>
> A great man dies: but one thing worse was spared;
> Not all his heart by their base hands lay bared.
> One comes to crown with praise the dust of death;
> And lo, through him this worst is brought to pass.

The real question for Swinburne (and largely for Matthew Arnold as well, as we shall see) is one of sexual propriety. The matter of Keats's masculine dignity, which Byron had long ago doubted and which Milnes had tried so hard to prove, had been raised again by the indecency of an editor who encouraged his readers to scrutinize the poet's naked heart.

Once the grave had been opened, Swinburne could not but look, and soon his indignation at the editor's act of desecration gave way to disgust at the scene revealed. Of the love letters he wrote, "If they ought never to have been published, it is no less certain that they ought never to have been written; that a manful kind of man or even a manly sort of boy, in his love-making or in his suffering, will not howl and snivel after such a lamentable fashion."[32] Henceforward, Swinburne's critical view of Keats hardened into formula. In the article that he wrote on Keats for the *Encyclopedia Britannica* of 1882 (which was reprinted well into the twentieth century), he calls the poetry of the first volume "the most vulgar and fulsome doggerel ever whimpered by a vapid and effeminate rhymester in the sickly stage of whelphood." This savage opprobrium matches anything in the "killing" critiques of *Blackwood's* and *The Quarterly*, as Swinburne reminds us in his judgment of a passage in *Endymion*: "Such nauseous and pitiful phrases as these, and certain passages in his correspondence, make us understand the most offensive imputations or insinuations levelled against the writer's manhood." With the publication of a slim volume of letters, the poet who had been "a man so perfect as Keats" was no longer even "a manly sort of boy." How is such a critical about-face possible?

One answer is that Swinburne has never been known as a consistent or evenhanded critic. Another might be the recitation of a proverb about pots and kettles: George Ford, for instance, reads Swinburne's stance as "the small man's passionate desire to assert his masculinity."[33] My aim here is neither to condemn Swinburne's critical powers nor to discount his judgment because of his failure to live up to his own standards. It is, rather, to understand those standards, and to show that biographical information (embodied in the letters to Fanny Brawne) catalyzed the statement of them. Clearly, Swinburne's image of Keats, transformed by the publication of the love letters, modified his estimation of the poetry. That Swinburne was not alone in his response to the personality of the poet is proven by an examination of a far greater critic and (in Ford's terms) a larger man, Matthew Arnold.

The essential ambivalence of Arnold's response to Keats was evident well before publication of the love letters. Nonetheless, he begins with biography. He read Milnes's *Life and Letters* in the autumn of 1848, apparently at the suggestion of his friend Arthur Hugh Clough, and wrote to Clough about the experience. "What a brute you were to tell me to read Keats'[s] Letters. However it is over now: and reflexion resumes her power over agitation."[34] Arnold does not explain what parts of Milnes's first selection of letters agitated him, but we can surmise: the sensitive young Victorian poet, who was in the process of transformation from the "Merry Matt" of undergraduate revels into the brooding moralist of *Empedocles on Etna*, was especially responsive to the life and letters of another young poet who had wrestled with many of the same questions. The trouble was that Keats seldom seemed to have wrestled enough. Throughout his career Arnold turned to Keats's life for illumination of this problem, and never completely mastered the agitation that it stirred.

"What harm he has done in English Poetry," Arnold wrote of Keats in the same early letter to Clough. To the eyes of a poet who believed that poetry itself must provide moral standards where an old order once stood, Keats, like Browning, had an insufficient "Idea of the world." If, as Arnold wrote to Clough, "modern poetry can only subsist by its *contents*," mere sensuous power and felicity of phrase are not enough. *Isabella* may contain more felicities than all of Sophocles (an extraordinary opinion), Arnold wrote in the preface to his *Poems* of 1853, but, lacking architectonic sense, it fails to present such an "Idea of the world"—fails to qualify, in the bolder terms the critic would later use, as a substitute for religion.

Given such exalted requirements, it is easy to see how Keats does not entirely satisfy. "Keats passionately gave himself up to a sensuous genius," Arnold asserts in his essay on Heine (*Essays in Criticism*, First Series). Again, in this image of Keats as a magnificent sensory mechanism, the issue of manliness intrudes. Hazlitt had long before found that the fault of the poetry was a certain "deficiency in masculine energy of style";[35] for Arnold, it was a matter not only of style but of temperament, and ultimately of conduct.

Arnold was genuinely divided on the question. Unlike Swinburne, he does not remonstrate violently over Keats's supposed effeminacy; indeed, before the publication of the love letters, he finds much of value in the Keatsian sensibility. Even in the 1865 essay on Maurice de Guérin, Arnold remains enough of a Romantic at heart to admire "the extraordinary delicacy of organization and susceptibility to impressions" in Keats's temperament; there is in Keats something healthy, "something genial, outward, and sensuous," as opposed to the inwardness of Guérin, which probably reminded the critic too much of the writer of *Empedocles*. Arnold was clearly attracted to the sensuous genius of Keats: it is this exquisite temperament, after all, that gives him a "natural magic" that approaches Shakespeare.

But Arnold could not rest in his longing for a Romantic appreciation of nature, for mere "susceptibility to impressions." (Keats could not rest so either, as *The Fall of Hyperion* shows especially; but Arnold, like many Victorian readers, either mistook the fragment for a discarded first draft or neglected it altogether.) In the outlook of the mid-nineteenth century, to remain at such a level, or to lament that one cannot remain there, is either unmanly or un-English, or both. Louis Étienne, a contemporary critic, offers this perspective from across the Channel: "Keats est peut-être le moins Anglais des poètes que la Grande Bretagne a produits dans notre siècle. Il manque de cette *manliness* dont le premier effet est de sortir du rêve stérile et de la plainte efféminée, d'accepter ce qu'elle ne peut [pas] changer et d'en tirer le meilleur parti possible."[36] That last phrase, with its essentially Arnoldian tone of stoic resignation, illuminates Arnold's judgment of the Keatsian temperament. Loaded with an exquisite sensitivity (a feminine quality that may be balanced by a "genial, outward" energy), that temperament remains largely passive (an irredeemably feminine quality). "Assuredly it is not in this temperament," Arnold affirms in the essay on Maurice de Guérin, "that the active virtues have their rise."

If Arnold sometimes seemed uncertain in his judgment of Keats, wavering between appreciation of the Romantic magic and condemnation of its moral inadequacy, the publication of the letters to Fanny Brawne tipped the scale. Although his earlier general references to Keats might often be interpreted as criticism of the poetry (the word "temperament" being applicable to both the work and the man), his commentary was now almost entirely focused on the character. Of course, the man and his work are not so easily separable in Arnold's broadly humanistic view: after all, the best poetry consists of "ideas applied to life." But the predominance of biographical commentary over textual analysis in the essay on Keats that Arnold wrote for Ward's *English Poets* in 1880—about four-fifths of the essay is about Keats's life and character—is unusual even for Arnold.

The essay "John Keats," which is Arnold's most substantial discussion of the subject and was included in the Second Series of *Essays in Criticism*, is an uneven performance, but a revealing one. It begins with an indictment of Keats's "sensuousness," which, as we have seen, was not always a negative quality in Arnold's earlier remarks. But after contemplating the passionate surrender of self in the love letters—"the abandonment of all reticence and all dignity," in Arnold's terms[37]—he was willing to believe the worst. His treatment of an anecdote about Keats provides an example. Back in 1853, the *Autobiography* of Benjamin Robert Haydon had been published, posthumously; it included a recollection of how Keats had been devastated by the critics. According to Haydon, he

> began to despond, flew to dissipation as a relief, which from a temporary elevation of spirits, plunged him into deeper & more inextricable despondency than ever. For six weeks he was scarcely sober, & once to shew what a Man of Genius does, to gratify his appetites, when once they get the better of him, he covered his tongue & throat as far as he could reach with Cayenne pepper, in order as he said to have the "delicious coolness of claret in all its glory!"[38]

It is highly unlikely that the story is literally true. If Haydon had seen such an episode, he would surely have told other friends, or at least recorded it in his *Diary*, but no similar account exists. As Bate comments, "It was exactly the kind of thing Keats might have been tempted to say he had done (or more probably was thinking of doing) when the humorless and teasable Haydon . . . was shaking his head."[39] In a letter to Clough (3 August 1853), Arnold also seemed to doubt the story: "Read the details about poor Keats at the end of Haydon's first and the beginning of his second vol. Haydon himself is a false *butcher*—revolting."[40] But there in the first paragraph of the essay written nearly thirty years later is the "cayenne pepper" story come home to roost, without a question about its source. "One is not much surprised," Arnold adds, with the credulity of offended hauteur, "when Haydon further tells us, of the hero of such a story, that once for six weeks together he was hardly ever sober." There is a difference, clearly, between the poet with exquisite "susceptibility to impressions" and the "merely sensuous man" who had written the letters to Fanny Brawne.

As the tone of the above judgment ("the hero of such a story") suggests, a large component of Arnold's reaction to the love letters is strictly social. Ever since the first sneering articles about the "Cockney School," Keats's undistinguished background had occasionally distracted his readers from seeing him whole; we recall the slightly misleading efforts of the aristocratic Milnes to heighten his obscure origins. Arnold's earlier conclusion that Keats lacked "moral profundity" had included a note of condescension toward the poet's intellect, but it required the letters to Fanny Brawne to provoke outright snobbery. After quoting at length from a letter that he found especially troubling—"My Creed is Love," Keats had declared to Fanny, "and you are its only tenet"—Arnold concludes, "One is tempted to say that Keats's love-letter is the love-letter of a surgeon's apprentice" (p. 103). And, so tempted, Arnold succumbs: on the next page he calls Keats a "sensuous man of a badly bred and badly trained sort" (p. 104).

In short, Keats's love letters demonstrate to Arnold that he was not a gentleman. In the estimation of the moralist who maintained that "conduct is three-fourths of human life," Keats the lover lacks the gentlemanly virtues of "character and self-control," which are requirements for "every kind of greatness" (p. 101). As James Russell Lowell had written long before the publication of the letters, commenting on the ferocity of Keats's early critics, "In England, especially, it is not pleasant to be ridiculous, even if you are a lord; but to be ridiculous and an apothecary at the same time, is almost as bad as it was formerly to be excommunicated."[41] The fact that among Keats's champions were eccentric Pre-Raphaelites like Dante Gabriel Rossetti, who had recently been branded as the headmaster of "the Fleshly School of Poetry," could hardly help. Ultimately, Arnold's 1880 judgment of Keats's character represents a coalescence of concerns both largely Victorian and specifically Arnoldian. Regardless of the concessions made at the end of the essay to the "elements of high character" that Keats possessed—lucidity, "flint and iron," and a spiritual appreciation of beauty that might, if ripened, transcend sensuousness—the damage was done. The dean of Victorian critics had spoken, and the image of a badly bred, self-indulgent, and morally dubious young poet was perpetuated. The end of the essay demonstrates Arnold's profound ambivalence about a poet whose "natural magic" had seeped into some of his own best verse.[42] That the surgeon's apprentice could finally be ranked with Shakespeare is a poignant reminder of what he might have done had he been properly bred and trained.

It is impossible to formulate a single "Victorian" image of a man so controversial as Keats. Each reader adopts the part of Keats—the outcast, the invalid, the lover, the surgeon's apprentice—that appeals to his temperament or fulfills his program. By 1880, however, it is possible to identify two main strands of reaction to the life and character. One, typified by Dante Gabriel Rossetti, is the pitiful view of the artist as pariah, which would culminate in Oscar Wilde's martyred saint of beauty. The other, represented by Matthew Arnold, sees Keats as a potential genius misguided by his own wayward inclinations. Both reactions are moral judgments, although Rossetti and the Aesthetes might balk at the label. And both are, naturally, inadequate views of the whole man. Two results all the responses had in common: they established Keats as a part of the late-Victorian consciousness about the poetic calling, and they posed new problems for ensuing biographers.

5
Among the English Poets
W. M. Rossetti and Sidney Colvin

'Tis good . . . that the Duke of Wellington
had a good Word or so in the Examiner. A
Man ought to have the Fame he deserves.
—Keats, in a letter to Haydon, 11 May 1817

For almost forty years after the publication of the first life of Keats, the biography of the poet consisted of Lord Houghton's new editions (amending some, but adding little), critical opinions of the poetry that touched on the poet's character (for instance, the Pre-Raphaelites' enthusiasm), critical opinions of the character that also noticed the poetry (especially reactions to the love letters), and outright legend based on the image of promise pathetically cut short. Suddenly, in 1887 two new full-scale biographies appeared, and an image became a literary institution. Following the work of William Michael Rossetti and Sidney Colvin, few readers could doubt that Keats belonged, if not with Shakespeare, at least "among the English Poets," as Keats had bravely hoped in an early letter to George and Georgiana (14 October 1818), when he had little reason to believe that the dream would come true. In 1848, some of Milnes's associates had questioned the value of research into such an obscure life; by the time that Colvin's second, larger study marked the beginning of a new period of Keats scholarship in 1917, Keats was one of the best-known subjects in English literary biography.

Although there was no new formal biography of Keats between 1848 and 1887, biography itself, of course, did not stand still. Two related developments especially prepared the way for late-Victorian biographers like Rossetti and Colvin. The popularity of literary biography continued to increase, spurred by an ever-growing audience of middle-class readers and by compelling public figures like Dickens, Disraeli, and Browning. And biography found inspiration in the novel, which had largely bred and nourished the new reading public. As moralists had long been fond of pointing out, biography could offer not only the suspenseful narrative and interesting characters of the novel; it had the added virtue of being based on actual fact.[1]

Indeed, biography has always been closely related to the novel—though often in the position of the poor cousin. When the English novel was developing in the eighteenth and early nineteenth centuries, from the supposedly factual accounts of Defoe to the historical canvases of Scott, biography was still primarily an appendage of history, linked in the way the "human interest" segment is to the nightly news broadcast. As writers like Thackeray, Dickens, and George Eliot led the novel more and more into the exploration of the individual's place in an increasingly complex society, so Carlyle insisted that biography could subsume history as an account of the struggle of "Freewill" against social constraints, a theory he tried to illustrate with the story of John Sterling's herioc battle.[2] Later, novelists like Henry James and Virginia Woolf would shift the focus of their craft to the hidden workings of the mind; twentieth-century biographers, also inspired by Freud, would make psychoanalysis an indispensable part of their research. I do not insist here upon a simple cause-and-effect relationship between the novel and biography, although it seems reasonable to assume that in most cases the scholars were following the lead of the creative artists in responding to the temper of their times. In the second half of the twentieth century, we may be witnessing a reversal of priorities, as biography continues to thrive on increasingly stronger standards and tools of analysis, while the novel appears befuddled, nearly refined out of existence by decades of innovation for its own sake.

But I anticipate. When William Michael Rossetti and Sidney Colvin were preparing their lives of Keats in the 1880s, the novel was still vigorously advancing new methods for biography. One of the most sorely needed developments was the notion of artful selectivity in biographical writing and editing. With a few notable exceptions—such as Carlyle's *Sterling* and Elizabeth Gaskell's *Charlotte Brontë*—nineteenth-century biographies had continued to emulate Boswell's example in their use of detail, but without his great subject or his dramatic power. The only reason for the relative brevity of Milnes's *Keats*, which proposed to tell its story in the subject's own words, was a scarcity of materials. Now, responding to the novelist's call for distillation and to the larger reading public's demand for cheaper editions, biographers began to place a premium on synthesis and selectivity, especially in the brief studies written for the new series of popular biographies, such as John Morley's "English Men of Letters."

Both Rossetti and Colvin wrote for series, which presented problems as well as advantages—as is usually the case when art or scholarship is institutionalized. The new format encouraged the biographer to compose rather than to compile, but it sometimes required the use of a Procrustean bed. When Morley wrote to assign Colvin an earlier volume in the "English Men of Letters" series (Colvin's *Landor* was published in 1881), he included this prescription: "Only let me petition you to give us plenty of the man himself, letters, talks, and personality generally. . . . Length, then, not less than 180 pp.—nor more than 200 pp."[3] It would not be easy to provide "plenty" of a long and active life within such sternly fenced bounds. Morley himself was able to write such a life of Burke, including a good deal of the historical and political background for the statesman's career, only because long periods of Burke's private life remained relatively unknown and his papers unavailable. In this regard, at least, the brevity of Keats's life was a blessing for his biographer.

We might expect that the late nineteenth-century novel would also bring to biography a greater naturalism, following French theories, in the fuller disclosure of detail about character and its environment. To a certain extent such disclosure did occur: Taine would have approved of Morley's sketches of intellectual history in his biographies of Voltaire (1871), Rousseau (1873), and Burke (1878), Dowden's reconstruction of the cultural surroundings in his *Shakspere* (1875), and Henry James's study of the Salem influences that haunted Hawthorne (1879). Moreover, by 1880 a definite tide of anti-"Victorianism" had risen, bringing in the notion that the mid-Victorian ethos of decency in biography might have been too fastidious after all.[4]

Nevertheless most English biographers remained reluctant to explore their subjects' secrets in print. For the most part, they shared a genuine distaste for the airing of dirty laundry and a distrust of theoretical speculation. Leslie Stephen, whose ground-breaking work on the *Dictionary of National Biography* helped establish new standards for biographical scholarship, voiced the characteristically English note of common sense:

> A little analysis of motive may be necessary here and there: when, for example, your hero has put his hand in somebody's pocket and you have to demonstrate that his conduct was due to sheer absence of mind. But you must always remember that a single concrete fact, or a saying into which a man has put his whole soul, is worth pages of psychological analysis.[5]

If the essential empiricism of the English character was not enough to keep late nineteenth-century biographers cautious, they were occasionally reminded of public expectations by the outcry that followed indiscreet disclosures. We have already seen how the publication of Keats's letters to Fanny Brawne in 1878 scandalized the most devoted Keatsians. James Anthony Froude provoked even greater furor with his four-volume *Life of Carlyle*, two volumes published in 1882 and two in 1884. The story of Carlyle and Froude is so well known that it need not be recounted in detail.[6] The essence of it is that Froude followed his master's policy of biographical candor so closely that many readers concluded he must have been Carlyle's enemy. He knew that Carlyle had long before excoriated English biography (in a review of Lockhart's *Scott*) for its "mealy-mouthed" delicacy, and he believed (rightly, in the long run) that his inclusion of what he calls "the prickly aspects" of Carlyle's career—the "natural irritability," the hypochondria, and especially the difficulties of marriage with Jane Welsh—would not only strengthen the biography but also do a service to its subject. Now that the worst was known, the world could gradually move towards a positive reassessment.

The reaction to Froude's work among other biographers—and, probably more important, among readers and publishers of biography—was immediate and vociferous. The household gods had been defiled, the biographer's position of trust betrayed, and whatever progress might have been developing towards greater candor was abruptly halted. The Poet Laureate responded, in "The Dead Prophet," using exactly the same tones he had used almost forty years before, when outraged by another act of biographical sacrilege.[7] Once again Tennyson sees the biographer as a vulture, abusing a helpless subject after "his friends had stript him bare."

> She gabbled, as she groped in the dead,
>   And all the people were pleased;
> "See, what a little heart," she said,
>   "And the liver is half-diseased!"

Such, then, was the atmosphere for literary biography when Rossetti and Colvin were preparing the first formal reconsideration of Keats's life in forty years. The genre had undoubtedly grown in stature, as new standards of scope and synthesis required more painstaking craftsmanship from biographers, but it still balanced precariously (as perhaps it always must) on a tightrope between discretion and disclosure.

Rossetti and Colvin started their studies of Keats independently, each at the invitation of a general editor for a series. As Rossetti explains in a

"Note" prefixed to his *Life of Keats*, his competitor published a week after he had consigned his own manuscript, and he had time to retrieve it only for the insertion of "such items of fresh information as were really needful for the true presentment" of his subject.[8] The coincidence of the two series calling for lives of Keats almost simultaneously marks his coming of age as a biographical subject with a rare chronological neatness. Because Colvin's work looks more toward the future, it will be convenient to consider Rossetti first.

The *Life of Keats* that William Michael Rossetti completed for the "Great Writers" series in 1887 offers yet another demonstration of the hinge-like importance of the letters to Fanny Brawne in Keats's reputation. Rossetti's acquaintance with Keats, of course, was born in the glow of the Pre-Raphaelites' admiration for one of their heroes. In 1872 he edited Keats's poetry for Moxon, writing an appreciative memoir that was largely, as he put it, "an abbreviated recast" of Houghton's study.[9] It portrays a virile, courageous Keats, full of "earnestness and pleasantry," whose flaws were only those of youth and energy—"a positive, not a negative, faultiness" (p. xxiii). Concerning Byron's "silly fable" about Keats's death by criticism, Rossetti concludes that "Lord Houghton has, to the deep satisfaction of all who value manliness as a portion of the poetic character, dispelled it once and forever" (p. xv). In 1878, just before the publication of the love letters, Rossetti reprinted this memoir, slightly revised, in his *Lives of Famous Poets*, which was devoted to writers "of widely diffused reputation"—again serving formal notice of Keats's ascendancy.

By 1887, when the letters to Fanny Brawne had become an inevitable part of the biography, Rossetti had begun to believe that a large portion of Keats's faultiness was undeniably negative. Finding in the letters a character "unbalanced, wayward, and profuse" (p. 45), he could not but change his estimate of the man, which, following Houghton's emphasis on masculinity, had been one-sided. Rather than analyze the letters and try to make room for them in a more comprehensive view of Keats, he apparently felt that further comment would only prolong the indiscretion, and preferred to look the other way. "Be it enough for us to know," he concludes, "that Keats, in the drear prospect of expatriation and death, wrote in this strain, and to wish it were otherwise" (p. 54).

But Rossetti's post-Forman judgment of Keats's character is evident even when he maintains silence on the letters themselves. Among the problems that the biographer of Keats—like most biographers—has to resolve is that of conflicting testimony from those who knew the subject in life. This task is especially difficult in the case of Keats, because his circle dissolved after his death into bitterly differing factions. Monckton Milnes avoided trouble, and gained a certain unity of impression, by drawing extensively on the memoir left him by Charles Brown. Before long, however, other old associates of Keats, inspired by Milnes's example, were putting their memories in print, making the biographer's materials both richer and harder to manage. A prime example is the disagreement between Haydon's *Autobiography* (published posthumously in 1853), which Rossetti followed closely, and Cowden Clarke's "Recollections" of Keats (in the *Atlantic Monthly* of 1861), which Colvin preferred to credit. Haydon claimed, as we have seen, that Keats "flew to dissipation" in his dejection over the reviews of *Endymion*; Clarke answered by calling Haydon "that ill-ordered being" and asserting that Keats never even purchased a bottle of claret, to his knowledge.[10]

Surely the truth lies somewhere in between the fading and distorted memories of Keats's old friends: we have already seen that Haydon's tales of cayenne pepper and six-week-long draughts of vintage are not to be trusted implicitly; yet we also know from Keats's letters that he enjoyed getting "a little tipsy" (letter to George and Georgiana, 16 April 1819) on claret from time to time. But, since Milnes had already made the most of Keats's available words, it naturally occurred to a new biographer to turn to fresh material for a new perspective. For Rossetti, who could not find the "unbalanced, wayward, and profuse" Keats of the love letters in Milnes, Haydon was the natural authority.

In part, Rossetti's view was a salutary corrective of Milnes's overly defensive emphasis on Keats's manliness. "Because he thrashed a butcher-boy, or was indignant at backbiting and meanness," the biographer reasons, "we are not to credit him with an unmingled fund of that toughness which distinguishes the English middle class" (p. 206). Such a correction, though, does not require swinging back into the arms of the excitable, unreliable Haydon, who concluded that Keats followed the flippant Leigh Hunt (Haydon's chief rival for Keats's affection in 1817–18) because "he had no decision of character" (p. 134). Rossetti qualifies this conception by appealing to Keats's unrealized potential—"He had within him the stuff of ample determination and high-mindedness"—but accepts the broad outline, judging that the "stuff" was "mingled however with deficient self-control" (a reasonable evaluation of some of the letters) "and with a perilous facility for seeing the seamy side of life" (pp. 138–39). This last judgment Rossetti leaves without proof—perhaps because he had none—in such a way as to suggest that the proof was unprintable. And it is but a step from this characterization to the final criticism of Keats's poetry: "most" of the poems, Rossetti writes, "amid all their beauty, have an adolescent and frequently a morbid tone, marking want of manful thew and sinew and of mental balance" (p. 208). In essence, Rossetti falls in line with the opinion expressed by Arnold and Swinburne after the publication of the letters to Fanny Brawne. In the 1872 memoir, he had praised above all Keats's "pleasantry" and power of youthful enjoyment; now, he finds the humor "forced or inept, wanting in fineness of taste and manner, and tending towards the vulgar" (p. 156). This attitude is the inevitable conclusion, perhaps, of a biographer who takes the humorless Haydon so seriously.

Rossetti does not always leave his statements about Keats's "vulgarity" dangling provocatively; occasionally he drops further hints. Of Fanny Brawne he shares the generally negative view that followed publication of the letters, but phrases it in a typically oblique fashion: "Miss Brawne enslaved him, but did not inspire him with that tender and boundless confidence which the accepted and engaged lover of a virtuous girl naturally feels" (p. 143). The reader is left to puzzle over this open-ended quasi-judgment. Did Keats lack "that tender and boundless confidence" because he was not accepted? because he was not engaged? or because his girl was not virtuous? Considering the paucity of information, the biographer simply couldn't say. But he has prompted us to question the beloved's virtue, and consequently, of course, Keats's taste in preferring her.

One further example of Rossetti's treatment of character—especially as it relates to sexual conduct—deserves mention here. Early in his biographical summary he makes note of the passing reference Keats dropped in a letter to Bailey on "the little mercury I have taken" (8 October 1817), and remarks, "It would appear that in Oxford Keats, in the heat of youthful blood, committed an indiscretion of which we do not know the details, nor need we give them if we knew them" (p. 23). The "indiscretion," which was first scrutinized by Sir Benjamin Ward Richardson in *The Aesclepiad* for April 1884, is here brought into biography for the first time (Milnes had excised it with an editorial pen), and has continued to fascinate biographers through Robert Gittings, who wrote an Appendix on "Keats and Venereal Disease" in 1968.[11] Again, Rossetti only calls attention to his discovery; presuming that the "details" would be too sordid to mention, he both avoids the burden of proof and provides another teasing sample of Keats's "waywardness." The suggestion may be true; but Rossetti's use of unexamined innuendo serves neither the reader nor the future biographer.

Ultimately, in spite of his Pre-Raphaelite background, Rossetti lacked sympathy with Keats; his own conclusion is that his favorite Shelley was "superior beyond any reasonable terms of comparison" (p. 208). But the biographer's chilliness to his subject is not fatal; after Milnes's sometimes uncritically appreciative *Life*, in fact, such a judicial approach is welcome. The deeper problem with Rossetti's study lies in his failure to impart some semblance of life within the constrained bounds of the series biography. His scheme—four independent sections that report in turn on the life, the works, the character, and finally the biographer's judgment of all—is simply mechanical. For example, in the first section (which devotes just fifty-two pages to the life, properly filling its quarter of the book), he mentions the publication of Keats's first volume in 1817, "of which more anon," postponing discussion until the appropriate section. This method certainly helps the biographer to organize his materials, but it gives the impression that the first volume, into which Keats emptied so much youthful hope, ambition, and apprehension, had nothing to do with his life, no impact on his character. In part, of course, Rossetti's room for effective arrangement of his materials was limited by an editor's demand for brevity; any biographer writing for a series confronts this problem. But a quick survey of other studies in the "Great Writers" series—Hall Caine's *Coleridge*, or William Sharp's *Shelley*, for instance—shows that they were not constrained to Rossetti's scheme of subdivision. To separate the parts of a biography in this way is not to recognize that Keats, like most creative writers, is of imagination—life, character, and works—all compact.

Sidney Colvin was more successful in almost every way. From the beginning of his *Keats*, where he names his fresh materials in the Preface, it is clear that his work is more scholarly than Rossetti's, more than an appreciative essay worked up for a series. Readers may still turn to Rossetti in search of a final Pre-Raphaelite commentary on Keats, or to investigate the origins of the reported venereal disease; but Colvin, whose study was reprinted fifteen times before being superseded by his own larger work of 1917, must be considered the authoritative nineteenth-century biographer of Keats. His monograph for the "English Men of Letters" series marks the point at which biography of Keats moves beyond belletristic survey and into the realm of scholarship.

Colvin's own background and circle of acquaintance certainly helped prepare him for the endeavor. By profession he was a critic of art: a friend of Burne-Jones and Dante Gabriel Rossetti, he championed the Pre-Raphaelites in Morley's *Fortnightly Review*; later, appointed Keeper of the Print Room at the British Museum, he cultivated an expert knowledge of Keats's pictorial sources, which have been further analyzed in this century in Ian Jack's *Keats and the Mirror of Art* (Oxford University Press, 1967). By avocation Colvin was a man of letters, a member of all the literary clubs and a friend of Morley and Stephen, Browning, Henley, and especially Robert Louis Stevenson. It was at the New Club (later called the Savile) that in 1869 he made the acquaintance of Lord Houghton, who was by then declining in years. Doubtless because of this association, Houghton's son, the Marquess of Crewe, later gave Colvin access to the collection of manuscripts that had gone into the making of the first *Life of Keats*. Colvin was thus the first scholar to be able to compare Milnes's *Life* to the sources, and his own financial means enabled him to purchase other important materials, such as the commonplace books of Keats's meticulous friend Richard Woodhouse, who carefully copied and annotated an abundance of Keatsiana.

Despite his scholarly opportunities, Sidney Colvin was not ready to take full advantage of the materials available for a truly definitive biography. In part, he may have been made cautious by recent controversy over Froude's *Carlyle*, controversy which was to continue into the twentieth century, in the form of bitter animadversion among descendants of the principals. But a large part of his reticence was strictly a matter of personal taste.

By way of explanation, let us consider another of Colvin's projects. Authorized by Robert Louis Stevenson, whom he called "for many years my closest friend,"[12] to edit Stevenson's letters, he completed the task in 1899, five years after his friend's death. In the preface he cited a passage from a codicil to Stevenson's will, as follows: "It is never worth while to inflict pain upon a snail for any literary purpose; and where events may appear to be favourable to me and contrary to others, I would rather be misunderstood than cause a pang to any one whom I have known" (p. xxvi). Colvin's comment, which recognizes the noble generosity of Stevenson's request, demonstrates his own uncertainty in such matters: "Whether an editor or a biographer would be justified in carrying out this principle to the full may perhaps be doubted." Nonetheless, this editor makes his position clear three pages later: "Much, of course, remains and ought to remain unprinted. Some of the outpourings of the early time are too sacred and intimate for publicity" (p. xxix).

Colvin's editorial stance is understandable; we have seen how, even in our own time of compulsively full biographical (if not autobiographical) disclosure, the executors of Auden have chosen to delay publication of an authorized biography until a decent interval after the poet's death. Nonetheless, we would be justifiably disturbed if Auden's editors were to resort to Colvin's method of getting the author's letters into print so soon after his death. As the modern editors of Stevenson's letters to Charles Baxter point out, the "majority" of Colvin's texts are "incomplete, frequently without marks of omission."[13] A striking example is Stevenson's letter of 2 February 1873 to Baxter, which describes the young man's anger at his parents' reaction to their discovery of his agnosticism. Without indicating an omission, Colvin deletes the bitterest passages, such as "I confess that I cannot exactly swallow my father's purpose of praying down continuous afflictions on my head," and "Charles Baxter, if you think it likely that you will ever beget a child, follow Origen's specific; it is painful, but there are worse pains in this world." Perhaps Colvin could not publish that last sentence, with its allusion to Origen's act of self-castration, because of prevailing standards of taste, but he might at least have indicated the omission, perhaps with an explanatory note; as it stands, much of the writer himself—the mixture of acid and jest, the crossing of anger and hurt affection—is edited out. With the manuscripts themselves under embargo by Sir Sidney's will until the middle of the twentieth century, the real Stevenson has emerged but slowly. Shortly before his death, he wrote to Baxter (26 March 1894), "Colvin (between ourselves) is a bit of an old wife." In a letter that the future editor never saw, he joked with William Ernest Henley about the kind of "Life" Colvin would probably write about him, sanitizing his riotous earlier days.[14]

My purpose here is not to demean the efforts of Colvin, who was a genuine and vastly helpful friend to Stevenson, but to show that his conception of friendship and posthumous loyalty was unfortunate for posterity's understanding of his subject. In some ways, his editorial relationship to Stevenson is quite similar to the position he had earlier taken as the biographer of Keats. As an established member of London's highest literary circle, he took the impetuous Stevenson, eight years his junior, under his godfatherly arm, and naturally took pleasure in the successes of his protégé. Later, he just as naturally remained protective about Stevenson's posthumous image, especially when it came to "the outpourings of the early time." He seems to have seen Keats in virtually the same light. The poet's early death made him, like Stevenson, a kind of perennial protégé whose errors, because they were excrescences of youth and not fundamental to his character, were to be either excused or simply erased. In his 1891 edition of Keats's letters, Colvin explains that Keats was "from the social point of view an unformed lad in the flush and rawness of youth." Reducing this opinion to absurdity, he concludes, "He never lived to be himself."[15]

Now it may be true (although some critics disagree even here) that Keats never fulfilled the potential signaled by his best work; indeed, virtually everything he wrote suggests that up until the final disease he was continually developing, both artistically and philosophically. Of course it is intriguing to ponder what he might have become had he survived, like his exact contemporary Carlyle, through most of the Victorian period. But the fact remains that he did not. We can study only what he was, and if we cannot call that "himself," then our language has no meaning.

The unspoken principle behind Colvin's opinion does, however, lead to a practical method for the biographer who sees that not all of his material supports his image of the subject. Instead of reporting the troublesome information and then qualifying it, showing it to be an aberration or relatively insignificant, as most modern biographers would feel bound to do, Colvin could simply ignore it as irrelevant to the real man, the man Keats would have been. The best evidence of this principle at work is in the edition of letters that he published in 1891. Here, he furnishes much more accurate texts than Milnes had done in 1848—he could hardly help doing so, after Buxton Forman's collected and corrected editions of 1883 and 1889—but he still excises, sometimes without warning, the parts of Keats's epistolary character that he considers not worthy of his ideal Keats.

First of all, the reader looks in vain for any of the letters to Fanny Brawne. In the preface to his 1887 monograph, Colvin had already recorded his dismay at their publication: "A biographer cannot ignore these letters now that they are published: but their publication must be regretted by all who hold that human respect and delicacy are due to the dead no less than to the living, and to genius no less than to obscurity."[16] A biographer cannot ignore the letters, to be sure; but an editor can, judging them a product of "the flush and rawness of youth." Confident that "charitable judgment will recognise that what was best in Keats was also what was most real" (*Letters*, p. xvii), Colvin simply finds the love letters too painful for print. He seems to hope that they will be forgotten, as he proposes that his should become the standard edition of the correspondence.

Besides his naiveté about the letters to Fanny Brawne, Colvin uses the editor's pen in one other significant way in the 1891 edition. He notes in the preface that he has omitted "a few passages of mere crudity" (p. xvii)—at least admitting that such passages exist, which is more than Monckton Milnes had done. Most of the time, he also inserts points of ellipsis where he has deleted something. For instance, in the letter to James Rice (24 March 1818), he includes a sentence that Milnes had omitted—"Some of the little Bar-maids look'd at me as if I knew Jem Rice"—and then deletes the rest of the passage, which begins, "One asked whether you preserved a secret she gave you on the nail." The lively letter to George and Tom describing parties, drinking, and "getting initiated into a little Cant" in the winter of 1817–18 (5 January 1818), which Milnes had chosen not to use, is included by Colvin, but he has Keats getting into "a little band," he relegates the drinking and gambling to a postscript (as if it were an afterthought), and he omits the bawdier sentences. His discretion is not surprising, nor is it terribly misleading: even Robert Gittings, who made an appendix of "Keats's Use of Bawdy" for his 1968 biography, had to concede that "Considering the manners of his time, Keats's letters and poems are remarkably free from sexual slang."[17] So Colvin is correct in his judgment that some half-dozen omissions will hardly distort our general image of Keats. The fact remains, though, that a part of the poet's character—a capacity for ribaldry, let us say, an interest in it, rather than a tendency to it—has been whitewashed. Sometimes Colvin's omissions seem to show that he himself was of two minds about the editing. In a passage to Reynolds about the social laxity of Milton's time (3 May 1818), he follows

Milnes in deleting "Codpieces" from the discussion, and then, curiously, almost reinstates the original text—"a hundred other disgraces"—by removing "social" from Milnes's "a hundred social disgraces." In sum, Colvin apparently desired a more accurate text than his predecessor, and he certainly achieved it, but his practice is still overly discreet by modern standards.

One more problem troubles the late-Victorian biographer: the knotty question of Keats's religion. Impressed as we are by Colvin's sympathetic descriptions of Keats's "manly spirit and sweetness," his "high good sense and spirit of honour," and his "warmth of sympathy" (pp. 212–13), we may miss the way the biographer glosses over, even distorts, his subject's irreligion. Milnes, as we have seen, diverted investigation by omitting some dubious passages and altering others. William Michael Rossetti added up the evidence—the poem on "Vulgar Superstition," anticlerical references in the letters, and the testimony of several associates—and concluded that Keats "was certainly not a Christian" (p. 157). Colvin preferred to summarize it all in two sentences, phrasing his conclusion so vaguely as to be misleading. "In religion," he writes, "Keats had been neither a believer nor a scoffer, respecting Christianity without calling himself a Christian, and by turns clinging to and drifting from the doctrine of immortality" (p. 206). This judgment, in its reflection of the vacillating nature of Keats's skepticism, is more or less accurate, although it ignores several stern comments in the letters on "the pious frauds of religion." But then Colvin, moved by Severns's piety at the deathbed, virtually administers extreme unction to the dying poet. In his nostalgic 1863 memoir, Severn included his wishful thought that Keats "died a Christian," inspired by readings of Jeremy Taylor's *Holy Living and Holy Dying* in the final days.[18] But in the letters that Severn had sent back to England at the time—letters that Milnes softened by deletion and that Colvin simply didn't print in 1891—the painter had recorded the agony of those days, which was compounded by Keats's knowledge that he was *not* dying a Christian. Abstracted from this material, Colvin's second sentence is accurate factually but misleading in its vagueness: "Contrasting now the behavior of the believer Severn with his own," Keats "acknowledged anew the power of the Christian teaching and example" (p. 206). To acknowledge the power of a creed is not necessarily to undergo a conversion, but Colvin's open-ended phrasing suggests such an episode without taking responsibility for it. In effect, Colvin's picture of Keats's final quietude is equivalent to the noble last words that Lockhart invented for the dying Scott.

In spite of his desire to ignore the passionately romantic, the ribald, and the irreligious sides of Keats, Colvin's 1887 biography is nonetheless admirable in many ways. He is more skillful in evaluating and integrating his materials than William Michael Rossetti had been. From the beginning he signals his doubt of the testimony of Haydon, describing the painter accurately, if superciliously, as "an artist who loved to lay his colours thick" (p. 3). Colvin is the first biographer to take note of the way Keats's letters to his sister, which were published in 1883, show "his character in its most attractive light," in that combination of frolicsome humor (which so troubled Rossetti), brotherly love, and almost paternal solicitude. Colvin also begins a reappraisal of Fanny Brawne: although he still believes that she did not realize what manner of man loved her (her letters to Fanny Keats, which suggest that she did know and appreciate Keats fully, did not come to light until the 1920s), he softens the harsh judgment of other Keatsians by citing for the first time her contribution to Medwin's *Life of Shelley* (1847), where she refuted the notion that Keats's temper was violent. Colvin takes pains to delineate the members of Keats's circle: where Rossetti dismissed Leigh Hunt as "too full of tricksy mannerisms, and petted byways" (p. 21), Colvin describes him and his influence in ten careful pages that show the mark of Morley's emphasis on intellectual background.

But the real distinction of Colvin's first *Keats*, as the discussion of Hunt suggests, is incorporation of literary criticism. Although the Romantic stress on personality encouraged the belief that a knowledge of the author was crucial to an understanding of the work, and vice versa, nineteenth-century biography never seemed very sure about the place of criticism.[19] The short shelf of Keats biography is typical. Milnes, whose primary purpose was to place the documents for a life before his readers' eyes, offered only occasional comments on the poetry in passing, most notably his judgment that most of Keats's poetic excesses are explained by an "indiscriminate reverence" for Spenser, "a great but unequal model."[20] Rossetti rightly pointed out that Hunt and earlier Spenserians like Mrs. Tighe were more important influences, and he gave nearly a quarter of his study to a judicial analysis of the poetry; but, as we have seen, his method of subdivision seems to separate the work from the life, effectively defeating the purpose of literary biography, which is to describe the cross-fertilization of character, circumstance, and tradition, to define the style that is the man.

If anything, Colvin devotes too much space to criticism—a natural resort when the life is short and the documents are still sketchy. But he integrates it chronologically, offering a well-tempered mixture of literary history and close reading. His judgments are generally more laudatory than those of Rossetti; in fact, he seems at times blinded by sympathy for his Romantic protégé. He finds the profusion of *Endymion*, for example, charmingly "Elizabethan," and the *Poems* of 1817, which Rossetti and others dismissed after admiring "Chapman's Homer," he praises for freshness and lyrical beauty. But he is usually clear-eyed enough to recognize Keats's flaws of excess, especially in the early poems; and he remains enough the High Victorian to wonder about the apparently amoral charm of the later poetry, for "under the influence of that charm both writer and reader are too apt to forget the need for human and moral truth: and without these no great literature can exist" (p. 160). In many ways Colvin's evaluation represents the culmination of the nineteenth-century progress of Keats's reputation: while reminding us of mid-Victorian doubts about the poet's character (Colvin resorts to Arnold's quasi-ethnic explanation of "Celtic instability"), he asserts that Keats was (again echoing Arnold) "the most Shaksperean spirit that has lived since Shakspere" (p. 218).

Sidney Colvin's 1887 *Keats* was to dominate biography of the poet for thirty years. Indeed, if we consider his 1917 volume an expansion of the same work, his authority extends to the publication of Amy Lowell's study in 1925, nearly equaling the thirty-nine years that Milnes's *Life* held sway. A few samples of critical reaction demonstrate its success. R. N. Prothero, the future editor of Byron's letters, wrote in the *Quarterly Review* that there was "little, or nothing" that the journal would change in its infamous 1818 review of *Endymion*, for the poem itself still merited such criticism. Prothero's portrait of the poet, though, is a remarkable testimony to the efforts of Milnes and Colvin: Keats was, says the unrepentant *Quarterly*, "unselfish, warmly sympathetic, proud, vehement, generous, incapable of meanness, full of common-sense and self-knowledge, distinguished as well for moral as for physical courage."[21] The critics were finally coming to agree with George Keats that his brother was "as much like 'Johnny Keats' as the Holy Ghost."

More significantly, even those who disagreed with Colvin's high estimate of the poetry no longer cavilled, for the most part, about biographical facts, about the poet's morbidity, his drinking, or his love letters. William John Courthope, himself a biographer of Addison and Pope, took strenuous exception to Colvin's conclusion that Keats was "Shakespearean" in spirit. His "absorbing pursuit of ideal beauty" through fairy realms is more Spenserian, says Courthope, who finds Keats incapable of "the more masculine style required for the drama, the epic, or even a stirring tale of sustained romantic action."[22] Such terms, of course, revive the discussion of Keats's manliness; but at least the criticism is based on the poetry rather than on biographical legend. This new emphasis is an achievement of good literary biography: settling and interpreting the facts as clearly as possible, it establishes a foundation for uncluttered discussion of the writer's work. In 1896 Robert Bridges could write critically about Keats's lack of humor and "true insight into human passion," and still conclude with conviction that the poet would be "loved and esteemed" for "the nobility of his character."[23]

To a certain extent, Colvin's revaluation of Keats represents a swing of the pendulum away from the critical judgments that mid-Victorians like Arnold and Swinburne passed on Keats's character. Like most attempts to bring contrary views to an equilibrium, it was itself exaggerated, insofar as it understated the extremes of emotion—passionate romance, bawdy humor, and irreverent skepticism—that made some late nineteenth-century readers uncomfortable. Generally speaking, because Colvin was more accurate than his predecessors, his influence on other commentators was felicitous. The only full-scale biography published between his two volumes, however, shows signs of a less fortunate impression. Albert Elmer Hancock's *John Keats* (1908), the first American biography, is for the most part an unremarkable re-telling of Colvin's material, with some attempt to paint scenes that would give his study "the dramatic vitality of fiction."[24] His basic conception of the poet, however, swings the pendulum even further in the direction Colvin had established. Where the earlier biographer had concluded that the reviews of 1818 were more irritating to Keats than devastating, Hancock claims that "the abusive criticism was one of the most fortunate influences in his career," for it created "a dramatic crisis in which he displayed his strength of character" by writing the great works of 1819 (pp. 108–9). Where Colvin had tried to establish the masculinity of Keats that sometimes vacillated in his "Celtic instability," Hancock admits no such wavering: "He was a man's man wholly. He loved to smoke. He drank wine with relish" (p. 111). Colvin himself knew better than to sketch his portrait in such unshaded black and white, and it would be unfair to blame Hancock's exaggerations entirely on him. But he was partly responsible, for other commentators did not have his access to original documents, and his distortions led to their extremes.

Colvin must have expected to have the final word by publishing the first really massive biography of Keats in 1917. One might hope that a comparison of this 600-page volume to the monograph of 1887 would clearly delineate the differences between early twentieth-century biography and its Victorian forebear, but in attitude and method Colvin's second effort essentially belongs to the nineteenth century. The real importance of the 1917 *John Keats* is manifest in its subtitle: *His Life and Poetry: His Friends, Critics, and After-Fame.* This book is not a new interpretation, or a deeper analysis of the poet in modern terms; it is above all an expansion of the 1887 essay, a "life and times" on the Morley model that is not limited to the format of Morley's series.

To say that Colvin's second study is essentially "nineteenth-century" in tone, however, is not to dismiss it as yesterday's news. For one thing, he had some fresh material. Since 1887, the original texts of Keats's journal letters to George and Georgiana had been recovered, filling in many important gaps in our knowledge of his doings and his philosophical preoccupations during the year of spectacular productivity between the fall of 1818 and the fall of 1819. Colvin was now able to clear up some old problems of dating (disproving, for instance, the notion that "Bright Star" was Keats's last poem), to extend his critical commentary (giving a full eighty pages to *Endymion*), and to expand his portraits of all the Keats circle. His new biography was by far the most comprehensive to date, and it seemed likely that any further work on such a brief life would consist of footnotes to Colvin.[25]

But Sir Sidney's great contribution would soon require more massive updating, for several reasons. First, as we shall see, a substantial number of original documents, including unpublished letters, had by now turned up in the hands of American collectors, who were eager to establish their own claims in the history of Keats biography. Second, Colvin's 1917 text is still expurgated in essentially the same way as it was in 1887, although all of the associates of Keats (and many of their immediate descendants) were long since dead. He is still of the opinion that the letters to Fanny Brawne are "too agonizing to read" (p. 464); working from his own edition of 1891, he still excises passages of questionable taste from the letters; and he still devotes just one short paragraph of the expanded study to Keats's religion, leaving the hint of a final inner conversion unchanged. Although most of Colvin's criticism is evenhanded and admirable, much of it has been transcribed directly from the 1887 essay (he admits to reprinting about forty-five pages, largely critical), and it sounds dated. For instance, his favorite major poem is still *Isabella*, which Keats himself eventually considered too sentimental, and he approvingly cites Lamb's justification for the preference: "To *us* an ounce of feeling is worth a pound of fancy" (p. 472). Finally, Colvin had the misfortune to be completing his monument to Keats just as profound changes were underway in society, art, and biography itself. At the end of his great work, which did as much as any since Milnes's to place Keats "among the English Poets," he wonders what will become of the Keatsian legacy in the modern world, after the Great War. He must have known that his own biography could not answer the question.

6
The Sympathetic Imagination
Amy Lowell

When we our betters see bearing our woes,
We scarcely think our miseries our foes.
—*King Lear*, III, vi, 100–01

Very soon after the publication of Sidney Colvin's second study of Keats, Lytton Strachey's *Eminent Victorians* (1918) fired the opening salvo of a new kind of biography that would, at least temporarily, obscure the old scholarly efforts in the flash and glare of its aggressively "modern" precepts and prose. Three years later, in the centennial of Keats's death, Amy Lowell started work on a lecture that would become the largest, most ambitious biography of the poet ever composed, sparing no effort to bring him to life in modern terms. These two works, though largely dissimilar, are linked by a common relative, the psychological novel. Together, they bring a century of Keats biography to a close, while opening for a new generation the question that Yeats posed: "Who knows his mind?"

Biography, like other branches of humane letters, naturally responds to the stimuli of circumstance. It is no accident that Lytton Strachey's collection of corrosive portraits, *Eminent Victorians*, appeared just at the end of the Great War that seemed to disprove much of what was believed eminent about Victorian culture. Like many modernists—Eliot, Pound, and Amy Lowell herself present similar examples—Strachey could no longer swallow the spoon-fed pieties of what he considered a hopelessly outmoded civilization. The Victorian period, he wrote, was "an age of barbarism and prudery, of nobility and cheapness, of satisfaction and desperation; an age in which everything was discovered and nothing was known; an age in which all the outlines were tremendous and all the details sordid; when gas-jets struggled feebly through the circumambient fog."[1] It was, in short, the best of times and the worst of times.

Clearly, though, for Lytton Strachey it was mostly the worst. Most crucial for the writing of biography, it was in Strachey's view an age deficient in the critical faculty. "The Victorian Age," he declared—he was fond of declaring generally about that vast period, as few careful scholars would now dare—"The Victorian Age, great in so many directions, was not great in criticism, in humour, in the realistic apprehension of life."[2] It is but a step from this judgment, which can be understood as the effort of a younger generation to cast off the cumbersome achievements of its progenitors, to Strachey's rejection of all Victorian biography in the preface to *Eminent Victorians*. Announcing at the start the polemical nature of his work, he scorns the "two fat volumes" of nineteenth-century biography, "their ill-digested masses of material, their slipshod style, their tone of tedious panegyric, their lamentable lack of selection, of detachment, of design."[3]

What Strachey requires from the modern biographer is nothing less than artistry. In his eagerness to deprecate Victorian forefathers, of course, he is unfair to biographers like Carlyle, Mrs. Gaskell, and Froude; nonetheless, it is true that their artistic achievements were exceptional, and that late nineteenth-century biography on the whole was in need of compression, scholarly detachment, and design. The efforts of the series like Morley's "English Men of Letters" to achieve these ends were motivated primarily by economic imperatives—the demand for small, affordable editions accessible to the growing reading public—rather than aesthetic aims. At last, Strachey proclaims, the time has come to recognize biography as one of the fine arts.

As in the late nineteenth century, the artistic form most analogous to biography—the *beau idéal* of the new biographer—was the novel. In the terms of Henry James, whose prefaces were helping to shape the way a generation thought about narrative, those overstuffed volumes of Victorian biography were "loose baggy monsters." Recognizing, as the modern novelist did in fiction, that no narrative can possibly be as objective as the mid-Victorian biography often claimed to be—we remember Monckton Milnes proposing that Keats tell his life in his own words—the modern biographer frequently turned to an indirect approach. Rather than pretending to the objectivity of the massive documentary study, he frankly declared himself mediator between the reader and the subject. In the novel, James's speculation promised new possibilities in the manipulation of "point of view." In biography, which is, after all, bound to the recording of fact rather than fiction, the new possibilities entailed the risk of new pitfalls. There is, no doubt, such a thing as a "creative" or a "cumulative" fact that may be reached only by conjecture and imagination. Biographical responsibility and tact often lie in the writer's recognition of the difference between the imaginative and the imaginary.

Eminent Victorians is virtually a study of the tensions between "objective" biography and the imaginative re-creation of a character; as such, it proves a useful guide, to the reading of biographies like Amy Lowell's *John Keats*. (Strachey's larger biography of Queen Victoria, published in 1921, is more directly comparable in scope to Lowell's project, but *Eminent Victorians* was the first bombshell of the "new" biography, offering a greater variety of perspectives on the genre.) None of the four Victorian figures under Strachey's scrutiny—Cardinal Manning, Florence Nightingale, Thomas Arnold, and General Gordon—is a literary figure, strictly speaking; yet Strachey's technique is so patently novelistic that his work remains highly pertinent to the history of literary biography. Many Victorian chronicles would have profited by following his basic procedure, which was to find a key to each character (a Jamesian "figure in the carpet"), and to elaborate it as a leitmotif throughout the portrait. More careful scholarship has shown that Strachey's keys—Cardinal Manning's worldly ambition, Miss Nightingale's bureaucratic ruthlessness, Thomas Arnold's pompous earnestness, and General Gordon's naive religiosity—reveal more about the biographer's anti-Victorian bias than they do about the Victorians themselves. But identifying a "ruling passion" (in the old eighteenth-century term), as Southey had done with Nelson's sense of honor a century before Strachey, was at least an attempt to give shape to an otherwise formless recital of events.

Strachey frequently uses the novelist's palette in achieving the broad brush strokes of his portraits. He creates symbols: "Cardinal Manning," for instance, ends with an emblem of the cleric's earthly ambition—the cardinal's hat, which hangs from his vault, covered in dust, "like some forlorn and forgotten trophy" (p. 114). He places his actors artfully, setting the manipulative, despotic Manning against the gentle, mystical Newman in a tour de force of contrapuntal characterization. He shamelessly combines provocative rhetoric and imaginary detail to create an impression. In one portrait he admits that his subject is fine-looking, "and yet—why was it?—was it in the lines of the mouth or the frown on the forehead?—it was hard to say, but it was unmistakable—there was a slightly puzzled look upon the face of Dr. Arnold" (p. 186). Nor does he hesitate to present another subject's interior monologue: "A thousand schemes, a thousand possibilities sprang to life in [General Gordon's] pullulating brain. A new intoxication carried him away" (p. 264). (This last scene comes shortly after a brief suggestion of the general's weakness for brandy.) Above all arches the narrator's recurrent and intrusive tone of satiric irony, as in his description of Hurrell Froude's religious conduct: "He was obsessed by the ideals of saintliness, and convinced of the supreme importance of not eating too much" (pp. 12–13).

The style of *Eminent Victorians* (more accurately, the *manner*) was imitated widely in biographical work of the nineteen twenties and thirties.[4] Strachey's fierce irony and iconoclastic rhetoric are entertaining at first, amusing for a time, and tiresome at last. Here is the modern agnostic's sarcastic reduction of the Oxford Movement: "Really to mean every word you said, when you repeated the Athanasian Creed! How wonderful! And what enticing and mysterious vistas burst upon the view! But then, those vistas, where were they leading to? Supposing—oh heavens!—supposing after all they were to lead to—!" (p. 21). So ends a chapter. As Newman Ivey White warns, "Cleverness and brilliance usually score points *for* the biographer and *against* his subject. The 'style' may indeed be the man, but too often not the man for whom the reader's interest has been engaged."[5] And in fact the man most clearly delineated in the pages of *Eminent Victorians* is Lytton Strachey, cleverness, brilliance, bias and all.

The manifest presence of bias might not have bothered the author himself, who apparently agreed with his friend Virginia Woolf's pronouncement on biography: "In order that the light of personality may shine through, facts must be manipulated."[6] Certainly the light of personality, which had not yet truly shone through in biographies of Keats, was an admirable goal; but Strachey seems not to have realized that his means to that end—distortion and suppression of facts that did not jibe with the aesthetic design—were essentially similar to the methods of the stuffy Victorian biographies that he deplored. Although the theories of Freud had started to affect the English-speaking world before World War I, Strachey's search for personality bears very little imprint of modern psychology: his portraits show virtually no interest in the infancy, youth, or family life of his subjects. (In fact, it was his imitators, participants in the "biography boom" of the twenties and thirties, who first started to give psychoanalysis a bad name in biography.)[7] For Strachey, personality remained a matter of biographical bas-relief, of isolating a character and artfully arranging a rhetorical setting around it.

Desmond MacCarthy, who first knew Lytton Strachey at Cambridge as a "long, limp, pale young man with pince-nez and a small rather dismal moustache," describes the Stracheyan dilemma succinctly: "A biographer is an artist who is on oath, and anyone who knows anything about artists, knows that that is almost a contradiction in terms."[8] The fact is that the author of *Eminent Victorians*, which was to have enormous influence on subsequent biographers, including Amy Lowell, was more an artist than a biographer. His ideal of Jamesian concentration and design was a salutary corrective for the worst of late-Victorian biography, and it would eventually bear fruit in lives that were both imaginative and accurate. His own work in *Eminent Victorians*, though, illustrates the necessary and desirable distinction between the novelist and the biographer. Henry James, who wanted to give his imagination free play, resisted hearing whole stories once he had identified the "germ" that inspired him to create a narrative pattern. The rest, he said, was only "clumsy Life at her stupid work."[9] For better or for worse, the whole story is what the biographer must hear.

In the midst of compiling her massive biography of Keats, Amy Lowell wrote to John Livingston Lowes, the chairman of the English Department at Harvard, "I have put Strachey up before me as a model, and I am crushed under the sense of my own incompetency."[10] She might well have felt crushed under the weight of her own materials for the biography, which made the emulation of Strachey improbable. In the same letter, she confidently explained, "When I finish my mountain of notes, the writing will be virtually done." Such an effort of comprehensiveness—Lowell perused more Keatsiana, much of it her own property, than anyone had yet seen—is surely not the method of *Eminent Victorians*. If Strachey is Jamesian in his selectivity and characterization, then Lowell, in the plenitude of her scope and the vital energy of her narrative drive, must be called Dickensian. Any biographer might have felt incompetent in the effort to reconcile the two. Both her successes and her failures are monumental, and they make her biography a landmark at the border of modern lives of the poet.

The story of the composition of Amy Lowell's *John Keats* itself approaches the quality of a novel, complete with a youthful infatuation, a cast of intriguing minor characters, and a heroic labor leading to untimely death. Her lifelong love of Keats (and no other word but "love" will serve) began when she was a teenager, introduced to the poet, appropriately enough, by Leigh Hunt, whose *Imagination and Fancy* first awakened her poetic sensibility. By the age of seventeen she had already formed the theory that Fanny Brawne had been mistreated by Victorian critics, and was really a sensitive, sensible girl worthy of her lover, rather than the heartless flirt of accepted opinion.[11] Lowell's first volume of poetry, *A Dome of Many-Coloured Glass* (1912), was drenched in Keats, from the title that she borrowed from *Adonais* to several poems of Keatsian inspiration, including a sonnet "To John Keats," which begins, "Great master! Boyish, sympathetic man!" When asked to deliver a centenary lecture at Yale in 1921, she was ready. And when the success of the lecture suggested some kind of book to follow, she eagerly accepted the opportunity to record, and perhaps to repay, her debt.

Despite Lowell's qualifications as a disciple, at the time a new biography of Keats seemed an unlikely endeavor. In 1917, most readers of Sidney Colvin's second study of Keats had judged it definitive; indeed, some expressed wonder that such a short and uneventful life had inspired such a long book. Considering Colvin's access to sources and his own long dedication to the task, the undertaking of a rival full-scale biography just four years later appeared positively foolhardy.

To her credit, Amy Lowell was nothing daunted by the risk of foolhardiness. She had her reasons for believing that there was a place for a new biography. First, she shared some of Lytton Strachey's animus against their Victorian forebears, although she seldom expressed it with his ironic scorn. Instead, she accented the positive side of the dialectic: seeing Keats as "an almost completely modern man," she insisted on a new perspective.[12] In the tug-of-words that she, like so many members of a younger generation trying to break free of older influences, rebelliously initiated, Sidney Colvin was the obvious opponent. She was largely right in her prefatory judgment (clearly aimed at the unnamed Colvin) that previous biographies belonged to the nineteenth century "in attitude if not in fact" (I, viii). As we have seen, Colvin was overly protective of his spiritual ward; his reticence regarding Keats's "raw youth" and romantic turmoil was simply outdated in an age that was gradually recognizing the value of full disclosure, at least in cases where no associates of the subject survived.[13] On the other hand, Lowell's private comments about Colvin—"the close-fistedest, narrow-mindedest man!" she exclaimed in a conversation with Louis Holman, "Opinionated old bird! I could scratch his eyes out!" (*Bostonians*, 86–87)— are far less fair and more indicative of her cantankerous desire for biographical battle.

Lowell never makes clear exactly what is "modern" about her Keats, but we may hazard some reasonable guesses. First of all, he was decidedly not Victorian. In a gesture that Northrop Frye has described as a search for a "modal grandfather," the biographer, like the more purely creative artist, may contemn all-too-familiar literary parents in favor of more distant, more easily loveable ancestors. Strachey's general fondness for the reasonable eighteenth century (compare his essays on Hume and Voltaire to any of his Victorian portraits) may be understood in this light. And Amy Lowell, child of Boston Brahmins who banned the licentious Shelley from the family library, raised on selected pieties from Gray and Cowper until she discovered Leigh Hunt for herself, seems to have found a personal analogue in the historical situation of Keats. "His life was one long, blind struggle to outdistance his mental environment," she writes appreciatively (I, 34). If the business of the modern artist was to cast off the trammels of Victorian convention (as Lowell had done in her eccentric flouting of proper Boston and her bold championship of new poetic technique), then Keats, who had scorned the old literary establishment in "Sleep and Poetry," had been ambushed by its rear guard in the reviews of *Endymion*, and then—unkindest cut—unjustly castigated by the hidebound Victorians, was a spiritual modern. Only someone who had gone the same steps as the author, Lowell implies, proving his experiences on modern pulses as Sir Sidney could not have done, could properly understand his struggle.

Not only was she, in her own survey of the historical terrain, a mental compatriot of Keats; she was herself a poet. "Critics don't know how a poet works," Lowell told Louis Holman in a pointed reference to her immediate predecessor (*Bostonians*, 86). Although readers of the past fifty years have not confirmed the judgment of her contemporaries, she was, when she undertook the biography, a poetic celebrity, known as well for her outspoken tracts and lectures about Imagism as she was for her small volumes of verse. She always claimed that she had learned more about the writing of poetry from the changes Keats made in the manuscript of *The Eve of St. Agnes* (which she owned) than from any other source, and she wanted to share a poet's perception of the poetic life. The danger in this admirable endeavor, as we shall see, was that she might not only revaluate Keats as a modern man but also remake him in her own imagism, as a Modernist poet, rather than a writer deeply engaged in the artistic concerns of his own time.

A more tangible reason for Lowell's presumptuous new biography lay in the fresh materials at her disposal. As a result of George Keats's American sojourn and the tenacity of American collectors, she had access to papers—most notably, her own collections and those of Fred Holland Day in Boston and the Morgan Library in New York—that British biographers had not seen. These included five relatively insignificant letters of Keats; several small scraps of verse (the completion of some partially published doggeral from a letter to Rice, eighteen lines cancelled from *Lamia*, an undistinguished sonnet written at Margate, and the dramatic fragment called "Gripus," now considered spurious); the biographical sketch that John Taylor obtained from Richard Abbey; some memorabilia of George and Tom Keats; five books from Keats's library, annotated in his hand; and an impressive gathering of drafts and manuscripts that promised to reveal the poet in the process of creation. All told, the new material, so much of it collateral rather than primary, might not seem to justify an entirely new biography, considering that Colvin had published on such large scale just four years before. Indeed, Lowell first proposed a smaller study, not strictly biographical, to be completed before the end of the centennial year, 1921 (*Bostonians*, 105). But she could not resist the desire to build rich garners for the grain she was gathering; in the end she could hardly control its ripening.

One more discovery by Lowell needs to be mentioned here, as it especially helps to explain another of her reasons for writing. Among the documents belonging to Mr. Fred Holland Day, a wealthy and eccentric collector of Keatsiana in Norwood, Massachusetts, was a series of letters by Fanny Brawne that he had purchased from the Spanish family of Fanny Keats, the recipient. In *Keats and the Bostonians* Rollins and Parrish tell the intriguing little story of the cat-and-mouse game that Day played with Lowell, allowing her to see just enough of the letters to convince her that her long-cherished theory of Fanny Brawne's essential nobility could be proven. Finally, after an exasperating campaign of letters and visits, she was given permission to publish extracts from ten of the letters, which do indeed demonstrate that Fanny Brawne was not, in Lowell's characteristic term, the "flibbertigibbet" that earlier commentators had maligned. A new biography, she believed, could clear the mist obscuring one of the keys to Keats's character, the great passion that had either baffled or embarrassed other critics.

To elucidate the meaning of all her new material, Lowell proposed an exercise in the new science of psychology: this was the final, overarching reason for composing the life on a grand scale, which would allow the light of personality to shine through the accumulation of incidents and observations. "Psychology has made great strides of late years," she wrote in one of the letters explaining her purposes to Day, "strides with which even Keats's recent biographer, Sir Sidney Colvin, has been unable to keep up" (*Bostonians*, 98). Later, commenting in the biography on Keats's early discomfort in the company of women, she wonders, "Keats's utter ignorance of what was the matter with him seems strange in this super-sexualized beginning of the twentieth century, when every school-boy babbles Freud" (II, 57). But her efforts at psychological explication are seldom as penetrating as Keats's own self-analysis in this case (a letter to Bailey, 18 July 1818), where he speculates that his "wrong feeling" towards women is related to the exaggerations of his "Boyish imagination." For instance, she judges from Abbey's dubious testimony that Keats's mother was "at once over-sexed and under-educated," and concludes, "That he sublimated her somewhat raw instincts through the medium of poetry into an ardour for sheer beauty, is a fact which should be easily understood by students of modern psychology" (I, 12, 13–14). This is hardly a fact; it is a speculative half-truth, interesting and suggestive but unrefined and unexplained by the biographer, who covers it in the cloak of "modern psychology." It leads her later to the assertion that "Keats never got over his need for a mother" (I, 76), which is either simply false or no more true of Keats than of anyone who loses a mother (depending on Lowell's exact meaning, which she never makes clear). This kind of conjecture is provocative, but it can tease us out of thought without establishing anything solid.

Fortunately for her readers, Lowell also possessed a sensible skepticism about the inchoate study of the subconscious that so captivated attention in the early part of this century. "To suppose," she wrote to a friend on the vogue of Freudianism, "that all life under the surface consists of violent sexual desires crushed out or sublimated, that all personal relation is a war of sexual antagonisms, is to see life through a perfectly distorted medium."[14] One only wishes that in the biography she had more often refrained from referring to Keats's "psychological processes," as if she were conducting a clinical study, when what she meant was his personality, or, more simply, his character. The unwieldy length of her study demonstrates a central problem of post-Freudian biography: what detail is relevant? Lowell considered "nothing which could clarify [Keats's] psychological processes too slight to be mentioned" (I, ix): we never know just what irritants created the pearl. But we cannot entirely blame her for using the vocabulary that she thought would appeal to the readers of her time, or for the chronological fact that the tools she wanted to grasp had not yet been refined for the uses of biography.

In fact, as in the case of Lytton Strachey, Lowell's occasional forays into psychology may tell us more about the author than it does about her subject. Almost all of the critics of her study noted the complex and obtrusive nature of her relationship to Keats, and with reason, for her own personality too often distracts us from her story. But, before we acknowledge the problems inherent in the biographer's personal involvement with the life she is recounting—even reliving, in a certain sense—we should remember the positive value of the process.

William Hazlitt, the critic Keats admired most, announced the essential precept by which Amy Lowell was to operate. In his *Essay on the Principles of Human Action* (1805), he rejected the idea, often stated in the eighteenth century, that all actions are motivated by self-interest. "I could not love myself," he explained, "if I were not capable of loving others."[15] Greatness in any realm requires what Keats was to call a "negative capability"; in Hazlitt's terms, it involves losing the sense of "our personal identity in some object dearer to us than ourselves."

The principle articulated by Hazlitt, which might be called sympathetic identification, or empathy, or, in a more capacious sense, sympathetic imagination, is naturally at the heart of good biography. As Shakespeare, whom both Hazlitt and Keats considered the greatest practitioner of this capability, was able to get beyond himself by embodying a multitude of ideas and emotions in the characters on his stage, so the biographer must transcend local limitations in order to share his subject's feelings, as far as possible, to see with his subject's eyes. Samuel Johnson described the principle at the outset of his main essay on biography: "All joy or sorrow for the happiness or calamities of others is produced by an act of the imagination, that realises the event however fictitious, or approximates it however remote, by placing us, for a time, in the condition of him whose fortune we contemplate; so that we feel, while the deception lasts, whatever motions would be excited by the same good or evil happening to ourselves."[16] The Romantics, less wary than Johnson about the dangers of imagination, would not always admit that the act of sympathy involves a "deception." Shelley's high-minded proclamation in *A Defence of Poetry* asserts the moral dimensions of the idea:

> The great secret of morals is love; or a going out of our own nature, and an identification of ourselves with the beautiful which exists in thought, action, or person, not our own. A man, to be greatly good, must imagine intensely and comprehensively; he must put himself in the place of another and of many others; the pains and pleasures of his species must become his own. The great instrument of moral good is the imagination.[17]

Like Hazlitt, Shelley defines the principle of sympathetic imagination as an act of love, which is clearly the motivating force of Amy Lowell. As Sir Walter Scott describes the emotion in simple terms but true:

> It is the secret sympathy,
> The silver link, the silken tie,
> Which heart to heart and mind to mind
> In body and in soul can bind.
>   (*The Lay of the Last Minstrel*, canto V)

Of course, the risks of indiscriminate application of such a principle in biography are manifold. The main problem with the sympathy expressed in Amy Lowell's *John Keats* is that it is not secret enough: the biographer is present on every page, in a variety of manifestations. First, as suggested in the discussion of her reasons for writing the biography, she identified with her subject as an artist, a poet whose career, in her view, was a struggle against outdated conventions and the *ancien régime* of insensitive critics. She seems to have found in Keats, whose magnificent poetry represents a victory over those enemies, the kind of suffering hero that Edgar discovered in Lear.

   Second, as many commentators have remarked, Lowell often appears to take the place of Keats's lost mother, the mother whose absence is so crucial to her view of the poet. Like the fatherly Colvin, she longs to protect the poor boy, but she lacks the tact of Colvin's scholarly, distant tone. Time and again, she cries out in her sympathy with his travails. Upon the death of his mother, for instance, when Keats hid under his schooldesk to conceal his chagrin, she exclaims, "Poor little shaver, so pitiably unable to cope with his first great sorrow!" (I, 14). We have no record of his reaction to being sent away to school, but the very lack of evidence is a goad to Lowell's imagination: "We do not need to be told," she writes, "that he stuffed his bed-clothes into his mouth so that no one should hear the sobs he could not control" (I, 24). Indeed we do not. When the biographer is this deeply engaged in the imaginative recovery of a lost or difficult time, pity may run too soon in gentle heart.

Finally, there are times when Lowell's complex affection for Keats seems more than motherly. As one unappreciative critic has suggested, the stout, ungainly, unpopular girl in her may have been attracted to the self-consciously short young poet because "he, among great English poets, stood most tragically for unfulfillment in love."[18] Indeed, her tone sometimes wanders from sympathetic attachment into the realm of sexual attraction. Using a Stracheyan technique, for example, she imagines the scene of Keats's composition of "Sleep and Poetry" in Leigh Hunt's study, surrounded by busts and portraits of literary masters: "Poetry! Poetry! That was at once his sword and the world it should conquer. But how still the room was, how breathlessly quiet and concentrated! How softly the night wrapped itself around him, how possible darkness made his wildest dreams! . . . So the night went, wide-eyed and exhausting; but the impression remained and out of it grew *Sleep and Poetry*" (I, 215). Where Strachey would turn the same exclamations and dramatic pauses to satiric account, Lowell gives us a dream-vision undeniably tinged with eroticism.

It requires no great subtlety to detect this undercurrent in the biography, for the biographer's insistence on Keats's youthful sexuality approaches an obsession. "Sexual love is the most stupendous fact of the universe," she declares (I, 364), and nowhere is it more stupendous than in *Endymion*. Lowell's fascination for that wayward romance—she devotes nearly one hundred and fifty pages to it—is the truest measure of her image of the poet. "With all its faults, obscurities, and digressions," she concedes, "*Endymion* is the spirit of youth rampant. Its adolescence is irresistible; to read it is to touch the dayspring of life" (I, 455-56). In her unveiled admiration for the poet of *Endymion*, Lowell practically reverses the stress of Sidney Colvin, who apologized for the "raw youth" of his subject; for her the young fellow dreaming of sexual fulfillment of the slopes of Latmos is the essential Keats. We have come full circle from mid-Victorian strictures against Keats's "unmanliness" to this "boyish sympathetic man" who is to be loved for his very boyishness.

Although Lowell's sympathy is a refreshing change from the scorn that Swinburne and Arnold heaped on essentially the same characteristics, it too can present obstacles to clear-sighted biography. The commentator who identifies too closely may engage in unwarranted compensation for the subject's apparent deficiencies, as Lowell does when defending Keats against the insinuation of an early associate (Henry Stephens) that he was haughty in his dedication to the noble calling of poetry. "But what a likable fellow he was!" she exclaims. "Who cares for his arrogance? Arrogance is inevitable when a young man is head and shoulders above his comrades" (I, 88). So eager is she to assert the superiority of her hero that she not only distorts a character trait by misreading a relationship (no other account considers Keats, so openhearted in most regards, arrogant—he was apparently just moving away from the more practical man Stephens); she also attributes to him a figurative stature that he never did achieve physically.

Excessive sympathy entails other misjudgments. Although Lowell's Keats is a plucky youth (in response to the dread reviews of *Endymion*, "he winced, but never for a moment did he flinch"), he is also a victim. In this view, of course, the reviewers Lockhart and Wilson are "first-class cads." More surprising to the reader of letters to, from, and about Keats, full as they are of the notes of friendship and of love, is Lowell's view of his intimate circle. She does not vilify George Keats for selfish duplicity in money matters, as Charles Brown once did; but (rather than reaching the more likely conclusion that John's financial fecklessness contributed to a mutual misunderstanding) clearly blames George for not explaining their problems to his brother. Benjamin Bailey, whose hospitality made possible one of Keats's happiest periods, the summer of 1818 at Oxford, and whose admitted bookishness helped inspire Keats to desire a more "extensive knowledge," she dismisses as pedantic and vulgar. She applauds Richard Woodhouse for his extraordinary devotion to Keatsiana, but finds his character pedantic and obtuse. (Lowell's desire to dissociate herself from the academic critics is manifest here, in her systematic disparagement of the more meticulous or scholarly of Keats's friends, those "unpoetical" creatures who are the poet's indispensable contacts to the ground of ordinary life.) The practical, orderly Charles Brown, who took Keats into his home at the death of Tom, gave him hearty company on the walking tour of Scotland, and tried to help repair his financial problems, however misguidedly, by proposing the botched collaboration of *Otho the Great*, is accused of "callousness" because in 1820 he followed his usual procedure of renting out his home while he went to Scotland, leaving Keats ill and unsettled. (The obvious explanation is that Brown, a creature of habit, did not know how desperately ill his friend was. Running underneath Lowell's deprecation of Brown, as of Bailey, is her disapproval of his alleged misconduct in a romantic affair. This judgment, which is speculative and peripheral to the matter at hand, should not color as it does her description of their warm friendship with Keats.) Finally, even the apparently blameless Joseph Severn comes under fire. In fact, the devaluation of Severn, whose deathbed dedication to Keats had become a sentimental legend in Victorian accounts, is second only to the restoration of Fanny Brawne among Lowell's revisions of the Keats circle. That he was "a weak and a vain man" is accurate, though uncharitable. But to conclude, as Lowell does (I, 106), that he merely "made capital" on the association with Keats is not just. He was not, it is true, one of the closest friends, and he may not have been as resolute and intelligent as later Keatsians could wish. But he was ready to make the sad journey to Rome on short notice, as no one else would, and he did stand loyally by the dying man, keeping a vigil for days on end, informing the other friends back in England in faithful journal letters. If at times he gave way to self-pity in those letters, and if he later took pride in his somewhat mistaken celebrity as Keats's great friend, it proves only that he was human, not that he was a self-aggrandizing leech. Amy Lowell's treatment of him, which borrows its petulance from Strachey, suggests nothing so much as envy of his position at Keats's side in the popular imagination. Her deprecation of so many of the poet's faithful friends serves two purposes: it prepares a place, by contrast, for the rise of Fanny Brawne, and it leaves the impression that only the sympathetic biographer can truly understand and appreciate her man.

At times, her sympathy predisposes Lowell to questionable reading of facts, or, more often, to the assumption of conjecture as fact. Although she is usually proud, in her hardheaded modernity, to resist the sentimentality of many mid-Victorian accounts of Keats, occasionally she succumbs. One irresistible source of pathos is Keats's illness—especially irresistible if at the time of writing the biographer is suffering, as Amy Lowell was, from debilitating conditions of sciatica, gastritis, hernia, and heart trouble. Using medical advice tendered by specialists to whom she had sent carefully prepared summaries of her view of Keats's health, she concludes that he had both pulmonary and laryngeal tuberculosis, starting as early as the late summer of 1817, when the ominously recurrent "sore throat" begins appearing in the letters (II, 359). More recent analysis inclines to place the inception of disease later—in the winter of 1818, when Keats was caring for his dying brother—and to locate the beginning of its active phase later yet—in the autumn of 1819.[19] Lowell's reading allows her to maintain two of her pet themes. First, it explains in part why the essential Keats of *Endymion* is obscured in the darkening vision of the later poems: disease clouded over the dayspring. Second, it renders the struggle and achievement of the last years all the more heroic, while helping to explain the passionate extremes of the love letters. Surely our knowledge of Keats's illness does help us keep these matters in perspective, but we should be wary of using it, as Lowell sometimes does, to explain away gestures or episodes that may not match our ideal image of the poet.

A related distortion by sympathy leads the biographer into one of her gravest critical errors. She essentially dismisses both versions of *Hyperion*, finding them uncharacteristic of the poet whose real voice speaks in *Endymion* and "La Belle Dame Sans Merci." Even if we admit that the severe style of *Hyperion* runs against the grain of Keats's talent, we should not neglect the significance of his undertaking the massive fragment and its revision; the very fact that he contemplated the project for so long makes it worthy of the biographer's attention. But Lowell doubts even the well-established facts of composition. Unable to accept that Keats was working on such an unnatural tour de force as *Hyperion* just before the great "characteristic" poems of Spring 1819, she postulates that he wrote the *Fall* first, drafting its apparently personal induction as a poetic response to the reviews of that year, and that he returned to the epic pastiche of *Hyperion* in the autumn of 1819, when he was attempting desperate remedies like *Otho* and *King Stephen*. Again, her overinvolvement with the younger Keats betrays her, for a misunderstanding of the two versions of *Hyperion* means a misjudgment of some of the most crucial autobiographical documents on the poet's late development.

Two remaining problems of Amy Lowell's *John Keats* are clearly related: style and size. It would be only too easy to multiply examples of her disturbingly intrusive editorial comments, several of which we have already seen as the result of her energetic sympathy. The essence of the style is one part Strachey, one part Lowellese. *Eminent Victorians* supplies the model for rhetoric such as her comment on the improvident Haydon's promise to his journal that Keats would "never want" as long as the painter, who actually drained Keats's small resources by ill-timed borrowing, could provide: "Fine words, Mr. Haydon, but how did you live up to them?" (I, 194). But if Strachey presented the model, the voice is unmistakably that of Amy Lowell, the enormous woman smoking black cigars while writing all night under an umbrella on an immense bed furnished with exactly sixteen pillows. It is a mixture of cliché, wandering syntax, coy colloquialism, and intense self-involvement. After describing one of Keats's agonized letters to Fanny Brawne, she concludes, "To the people who object to this side of Keats, we can only say, 'Love me, love my dog' " (II, 141–42).

The inordinate length of her biography (thirteen hundred pages) is a natural result of such vigorous prolixity. Another cause is the desire, noted above, to include everything that might clarify Keats's "psychological processes." This desire is naturally linked to Lowell's need to justify her own study, coming as it does so soon after Colvin's large biography. Thus she gives us reams of data and discovery, such as that "most important document," Keats's passport for Italy (reproduced in two photographs), and twenty pages on possible links between Keats and Drayton, as background for *Endymion*. Ultimately, the two large volumes read like the long draft of a biography, full of the biographer's questions, notes to herself, and explorations of possibilities rejected—all the seams of the process. This method of work-in-progress—if it can be called a method—is sometimes valuable for later researchers, who can follow every bend of her thought, but it is very hard to read. It is, as Conrad Aiken lamented in an unfavorable review, "a miracle of dimensions," like "the largest potato at the Fair."[20]

For all the flaws of its extravagance, Lowell's *Keats* also possesses many of the virtues attendant on energy and conviction. Although it has been superseded, it was a valuable sourcebook when published. At times the raw material wants digesting, as when she presents eight pages of quotation from Chapman's *Homer* and Robertson's *History of America* for the background of a sonnet; at times it wants discarding, as when she sidetracks to Edgar Allan Poe and decides to "follow, just for fun, his indebtedness to Keats" (I, 593). But this rough matter sits side by side with previously unpublished letters and drafts of poems like *The Eve of St. Agnes,* showing the poet in the midst of composition. As Johnson said, it is easier to take away superfluities than to supply defects. We may regret the biographer's unwillingness to select from the mountain of notes, but the result, in its amplitude, is something like life at her clumsy work.

Beyond its sheer bulk of information, Lowell's biography also makes important advances over previous estimates of Keats's character. She appreciates his humor and recognizes his occasional bawdiness as no biographer had done before, accurately citing the few stories on his drinking and noting that the rare sexual pleasantries in the letters were addressed only to his brothers and ribald friends like James Rice. And she frankly acknowledges his religious skepticism (I, 497-98), as Colvin had been unwilling to do. In fact, she not only prints everything that earlier biographers had omitted about his thoughts of suicide, but she expresses outrage that the religious scruples of Severn and Dr. Clark would not grant Keats his wish for release from suffering by laudanum (II, 523). Here, as everywhere in *John Keats*, Lowell's personal involvement intrudes on the story; but at least she tells the story with a completeness and honesty previously unattained.

Finally, Lowell largely achieves one of her primary goals—the restoration of favor, and some depth, to Fanny Brawne. With the help of the letters she cajoled from Fred Holland Day, she resurrects Keats's beloved as a girl of "no mean mental abilities," flirtatious but sensible and caring (II, 129). Although the excerpts that Lowell prints are inconclusive, the letters show that Fanny's attachment to Keats was much deeper and more enduring than critics like Sir Charles Dilke had suggested. They also support the biographer's claims for Fanny's intelligence and firmness of character. Not only was she thoroughly devoted to Keats; her lively imagination and solid education suggested that she would have made him a good wife. When the thirty-one letters to Fanny Keats were published in their entirety in 1936, they justified Amy Lowell's faith.

In the process of raising Fanny Brawne, Lowell demonstrates the flexibility of her sympathy with Keats, for she must concede that "he wronged her far more seriously than she ever wronged him" (II, 133). "Let us admit, once and for all," Lowell wisely concludes, "that Keats must have been a very uneasy lover" (II, 180). This fresh awareness lends her study an unprecedented depth in its consideration of one of the crucial questions about Keats's inner life: how can we account for the outburst of genius represented by the poems of early 1819? Sidney Colvin did little to explain it, but judged that the dry month from mid-February to mid-March was the result of the disturbing proximity of Fanny, who was next door under the same roof. Lowell's conclusion, that the great poetry was a direct result of happy affection, may not be entirely accurate either, in its simplistic disregard for the usual vacillations of hope and fear in first love, and of other matters, like Keats's relationship to past poets. Nonetheless, it raises new possibilities, and her recognition of the "empty" month as a naturally fallow period rings true. The question must remain unanswered—Freud himself admitted that "before the problem of the creative artist, analysis must lay down its arms"[21]—but Lowell, by recovering some of the contours of Keats's one great passion, brings us closer to understanding the question's terms.

Amy Lowell probably would have called her biography of Keats a "labor of love": it ever the cliché were appropriate, it would be for this effort. In 1922 she lamented the "pure drudgery" of it, admitting (in a letter to Elsie Sargent) that she "was not made for a scholar."[22] A year later, she confided to John Gould Fletcher that the biography was "a terrible piece of work. I never ground at anything so hard, it is two years now since I began doing it, and if I do not get to the end soon I shall sink into my grave and order the unfinished manuscript raised over me as a cenotaph" (*Bostonians*, 30). In 1924 she wrote to Louis Untermeyer, "Keats is nearly killing me, and that's a fact."[23] She was hardly exaggerating. Just three months after the publication of her study (in February, 1925), exhausted by her travail though exhilarated by its early success—it was an immediate bestseller—she died of a stroke.

The critical reception of the project to which Lowell devoted so much of herself makes an intriguing postscript. In America, the response was almost entirely positive (we have seen the exception of Conrad Aiken), praising her for her modern use of materials, her medical and psychological sophistication.[24] English reviewers were nearly as united in their disapproval. Edmund Gosse (a friend of Sidney Colvin) went so far as to doubt the authenticity of the one large contribution they all had to admit—the new letters of Fanny Brawne—as he sniffed about "the stuff which comes back to us, supplied to American collectors from no one knows what secret sources."[25] But then, "American collectors are easily carried off their legs." Anyone who knew Amy Lowell knew that this snobbish statement was true neither figuratively nor literally. Later in the year another English commentator who was overly fond of dramatic parallels suggested that Lowell herself had been killed by the critics.[26]

Happily, the days of nationalistic sniping among readers of Keats are over, and the enormous collection of materials that Amy Lowell left to the Houghton Library at Harvard has been analyzed with signal merit by the ensuing generations of American scholars. Lowell's life of Keats has been superseded, of course: she herself supposed that each generation would have to rewrite the biographies of major figures in its own terms. But her work retains a prominent place among all the materials, a monument to her boldness and the vigor of her commitment. Compared to the work of her model, Lytton Strachey, her biography may seem formless, unsophisticated, and too simply appreciative. But it stands as proof of William James's wisdom in his essay on "The Social Value of the College-Bred." "Real culture," he maintained, "lives by sympathies and admirations, not by dislikes and disdains; under all misleading wrappings it pounces unerringly upon the human core."[27] Amy Lowell may have loved not wisely but too well. But there is no doubt that she imagined intensely and comprehensively.

Epilogue

"Never say you know the final word about any human heart!" The opening sentence of Henry James's story "Louisa Pallant" might stand as an admonition to any biographer, be he never so well armed with "authoritative" documents and the latest theories of human development. The burgeoning of biographical study on Keats since the death of Amy Lowell suggests nothing so clearly as the recognition that the final word has yet to be said.

By and large, Keats has been happy in his modern biographers. Although Sidney Colvin and Amy Lowell did much to establish the twentieth-century view of the poet, subsequent scholarship has clarified many questions and strengthened his position among the highest rank of English writers. Since the beginning of his fame in the mid-nineteenth century, Keats's reputation has never suffered a period of general disfavor; in fact, it has steadily grown, and his biographers may be as important as any other force behind the rise to prominence.

The one common thread linking the biographies of the past sixty years is, as we might expect, improved scholarship. At the center of our increasingly clear view of Keats stands the magisterial editorial achievement of Hyder Edward Rollins. In 1948, the centennial of Milnes's *Life*, Rollins combined the material gathered by the first biographer (the Crewe Collection) with the collection of Amy Lowell and the manuscripts of Richard Woodhouse (now in the Pierpont Morgan Library of New York) into his invaluable sourcebook on Keats's family and friends, *The Keats Circle*. In 1958, he completed and corrected the long labors of Harry Buxton Forman and his son Maurice by publishing a new edition of Keats's letters. Given this fresh textual foundation, Keats biography flourished in the following decade.

A brief look at the three large-scale biographies of Keats in the 1960s may suggest the directions of recent work on the poet's life. (Aileen Ward and W. J. Bate published two weeks apart in 1963, and Robert Gittings in 1968.) Before allowing the inevitable and odious comparisons, though, it should be noted that all three are tributes to the advances of biographical scholarship, all superior to any biography published before this decade. Founded on a more thorough understanding of texts and dates, these lives demonstrate the modern fascination for the phenomenon of Keats's *development* as a poet and as a man—a phenomenon that Amy Lowell, for all the epic scope of her work, hardly suggested. No longer does the biographer of Keats attempt to identify a "ruling passion" or a single image, such as Milnes's manly striver, Colvin's unformed youth, or Lowell's boyish man. Instead, working with better texts and more fluid notions of personality, modern biographers have refined the portrait by stressing the growth of the poet's mind.

The natural result of improved scholarship has been greater subtlety, accuracy, and sensitivity to circumstances. But among the gains one danger should be signaled. In our focus on Keats's astonishingly rapid development, we tend to emphasize what he was becoming rather than what he was. We see the deepening speculation, the maturing character, and above all the splendid poetry of 1819, and, naturally preferring them to the earlier evidence of confusion and sentimentality, we may neglect a large portion of Keats's life and works. We are right to concentrate on what is best in him, for it is most rewarding; as Bate remarks, all writers may take courage at the example of his growth from embarrassing immaturity to unquestionable mastery.[1] But we should not forget that the embarrassing passages are a part, and a large part, of the whole man.

The subtitle of Aileen Ward's *John Keats: The Making of a Poet* signals her controlling interest in the development of personality. Reversing the classical dictum that *poeta nascitur non fit*, she proposes to demonstrate the process of Keats "making himself a poet."[2] Her authority for the study is Otto Rank, the protégé of Freud whose application of psychoanalysis to the creative character (*Der Künstler*, 1907) was expanded and published in English as *Art and Artist: Creative Urge and Personality Development* in 1932. Some of the resultant ideas recall Amy Lowell's psychological speculations. Most centrally, according to Ward, Keats suffered from an "insoluble conflict of emotions about his mother" (p. 10). Traumatized by her rapid remarriage after his father's death, the young Keats desperately sought a father figure in older friends like Cowden Clarke and Leigh Hunt, and (more speculatively) always distrusted women—a view that might explain his anguished suspicions about Fanny Brawne in letters of the final year.

Such speculation is usefully provocative, when proposed as conjecture and not stated as fact. But the psychoanalytical biographer's desire to reconstruct a personality too often leads to a certainty based on someone's else's paradigm, and, as with Amy Lowell, an inclination to recreate likely scenes that hold together the theoretic structure of the life. Ward's narrative abounds with assertions that Keats "must have" done so and so, or, worse, thought such and such, at particular moments. A favorite novelistic device is the creation of tableaux hinted at in the letters or the poems, such as the following idylls: "The blueness of noon seemed to smile down on him, and the faces of the dead peered out of the clouds at sunset; he lay awake at night, staring up at the stars, which seemed to gaze unblinkingly down on the earth below" (p. 26). This reconstruction is not too far from Amy Lowell's breathless description of the young Keats's sleepless night at Leigh Hunt's home. Doubtless Keats did pass such moments of splendor in the grass, but to state how they *seemed* to him, without direct warrant from his writings, is to create imaginary details that can only be called sentimental.

Ward's emphasis on the visual scene typifies her approach to the poetry as well. Like many literary critics of the mid-twentieth century, she focuses on imagery and metaphor, often using them as indices of development, illustrating trends of thought with threads of figurative language from the poems. When not stretched too far (for instance, to the point where Moneta=the Goddess of Melancholy=La Belle Dame=Lamia=the Bright Star=the moon of *Endymion*=Keats's dead mother, "shrouded in her coffin" on page 340), this practice enlightens both the poetry and the life, as it links recurring preoccupations and charts their progress over time. But for a study of Keats, whose poetry calls into play so much more than imagery—matters such as meter, sound, form, and response to literary tradition—this kind of criticism remains severely limited. Ultimately, Ward's study makes its place as a "popular" biography that does not scant scholarship, a lively narrative for the reader more concerned with the life than the works.

Walter Jackson Bate's achievement in his *John Keats* is more capacious. First and foremost, it is a critical biography, a literary biography in the tradition founded by Johnson's *Lives of the Poets*. The approach, which blends biographical detail and literary criticism with more grace and authority than any other study of Keats, suits its subject especially well. In some biographies the massive attention Bate gives to matters of literary context and technique might seem extraneous, more appropriate to exclusively critical studies like his earlier work, *The Stylistic Development of Keats* (1945). His frequent excursions into criticism might disrupt the narrative in such a way as to distract the reader from events in the life. But Keats was so deeply and emotionally engaged in a quest to take his place in the pantheon of English poets that the literary tradition itself becomes a crucial fact of his career. So consuming was his study of masters like Spenser, Shakespeare, Milton, and Dryden that we might say (echoing a phrase he admired in Chapman's Homer) that they "soaked his heart through." Only by the study of so-called "technical" details like those Bate provides—examination of stanza form, meter, caesural pauses, and repetition of sounds, among many concerns that mattered more to Keats than they do to most modern readers—can we begin to understand his effort.

For all his concentration on Keats's literary achievement, Bate does not neglect biographical details and the analysis of character. His portrait of a robust, good-humored young man devoted to poetry and buffeting with baleful circumstance represents the fruition of modern tendencies in Keats biography. He clarifies our vision of Keats's relationships with important figures like his brother George, Richard Abbey, and Charles Brown. (Aileen Ward conceives of Brown as a selfish cad, motivated mostly by dishonorable sexual drives; Bate's picture of a practical and loyal if shallow friend appears more lifelike.) And he offers special insight into the psychology of what he has since called "the burden of the past"—the poet's sense of futility when faced with the intimidating example of earlier writers' accomplishments.

For other kinds of modern research into personality Bate has less patience. His concern is not so much with Keats's psychic origins and "formative" experiences in childhood (the record of which is shadowy at best) as with the conscious attempt to shape a career out of influences, sometimes in opposition to them. "Possibly our legacy from Freud and from the historical approach of the nineteenth century," he writes, "encourages us to concentrate too exclusively on what we conceive to be origins and to neglect the psychological effects of efforts and ideals."[3] By focusing on Keats's dedication to poetic grandeur, Bate presents an inspiring argument for free agency, against all forms of determinism. Where Ward's model was Otto Rank, Bate's is the twentieth-century philosopher Alfred North Whitehead, who declared, "Moral education is impossible apart from the habitual vision of greatness."[4]

Finally, five years later, Robert Gittings published a full-scale biography that represents the culmination of his own long-lived fascination with Keatsiana. His four previous books and many articles on Keats had purchased Gittings a small notoriety for outspoken and uncommon interpretations of details in the life. One of his premises was the notion that before describing anything, Keats must have either visited the scene or else opened an appropriate book for immediate reference, as if he possessed neither imagination nor memory.[5] Gittings built this premise into his requirements for the ideal biographer, who must follow Keats's steps and peruse every document available. Such rigor led him to a certain amount of carping with his competitors; for instance, he declared in a review that "Bate brings nothing new to Keats's biography," because "what is needed in any 'new' biography of such a well-known figure as Keats is the historian's use of first-hand documentary material."[6] Later, in the introduction to his own biography, as he attempts to justify another such chronicle, he claims to have fulfilled the requirements: "I have personally seen more of the original sources for a life of Keats than anyone now living."[7]

To his credit, Gittings does bring a good deal of new detail to the biography. He offers many useful emendations and additions on dates, financial matters, Keats's origins, and things Keats probably saw, such as the chapel at Stansted that may have informed his settings for *The Eve of St. Agnes* and *The Eve of St. Mark*. The 1968 biography is more cautious, less aggressively speculative than Gittings's earlier works. Where he had once insisted that "Bright Star" was inspired by Mrs. Isabella Jones (whose name Gittings had made controversial in his previous books), now he allows that the sonnet may portray a general tension of romantic feelings rather than a specific romance (p. 264). His study is, as Jack Stillinger puts it, the first "American" biography of Keats written by an Englishman—a meticulous and comprehensive consideration of fact and document, as opposed to the more leisurely essay typical of English biography.[8]

Still, Gittings's portrait is not, as he claims, "on many counts a new view of Keats." He offers a slight (and salutary) adjustment of the lens on what Keats called his "horrid Morbidity," which was somewhat obscured in Bate's effort to stress the young man's healthy-minded vigor. But the real contribution of Gittings's biography lies in a significant collection of corrected dates and details, not in a new image of the poet. His gathering of evidence on such matters as venereal disease, "Keats's bawdy," and the importance of Isabella Jones may appear dubious to many Keats scholars, but it shows at least that there remains room for further discussion, discovery, and reinterpretation of even such a well-known life.

In a letter to Benjamin Bailey (22 November 1817), Keats included a "favorite speculation" on life after death—"that we shall enjoy ourselves here after by having what we called happiness on Earth repeated in a finer tone." One of the causes for his happiness on earth (and also a source of anxiety, as we have seen) was the bright dream of poetic fame. The development of Keats biography has helped to fulfill his dream, by repeating the life in ever finer tones. Ultimately, the poet's biography must consist of more than one life, for no single biographer can seize the man in all his moments. Instead, the Keats we know today is the sum of all the lives of the poet, from Shelley's "pale flower" to the modern biographer's sensible craftsman. We may not yet know his mind, but, thanks to the biographers, we better understand his experiment in living.

Notes

PROLOGUE

¹ *Rambler* Number 60, in *Selected Essays from the "Rambler," "Adventurer," and "Idler,"* ed. Walter Jackson Bate (New Haven: Yale University Press, 1968), 110.
² Unpublished lecture, quoted in Richard Ellman, *Yeats: The Man and the Masks* (London: MacMillan and Co., 1949), 5.
³ "Biography," in *Poems* (New York: Macmillan, 1960), 192.

CHAPTER 1

¹ Jack Stillinger, ed., *The Poems of John Keats* (Cambridge: Harvard University Press, 1978), pp. 102-3.
² See James L. Clifford, "How Much Should a Biographer tell? Some Eighteenth-Century Views," in *Essays in Eighteenth-Century Biography*, ed. Philip B. Daghlian (Bloomington, Ind.: University of Indiana Press, 1968), pp. 67-95.
³ *The Invention of the Self: The Hinge of Consciousness in the Eighteenth Century* (Carbondale, Ill.: Southern Illinois University Press, 1978).
⁴ "Biography," *Critical and Miscellaneous Essays* (London: Chapman and Hall, 1899), 3:46.
⁵ James Clifford, "Introduction" to *Twentieth-Century Interpretations of Boswell's "Life of Johnson"* (Englewood Cliffs, N. J.: Prentice-Hall, 1970), p. 15.
⁶ *The Prose Works of William Wordsworth*, ed. W. J. B. Owen and Jane Worthington Smyser (Oxford: Clarendon Press, 1974), 3:121, 126.
⁷ Quoted in Richard D. Altick, *Lives and Letters: A History of Literary Biography in England and America* (New York: Alfred A. Knopf, 1965), 90n.
⁸ "Modern Biography," an unsigned article, *Blackwood's Edinburgh Magazine* 65 (February 1849), 221.
⁹ See Francis R. Hart, "Boswell and the Romantics: A Chapter in the History of Biographical Theory," *ELH* 27 (March 1960), 44-65.

[10] For a fuller discussion, see Joseph W. Reed, Jr., *English Biography in the Early Nineteenth Century* (New Haven: Yale University Press, 1966).

[11] The inclusion of letters in biography was, of course, no guarantee of lively immediacy: Johnson pronounced Mason's *Gray* "mighty dull."

[12] *Annual Review* 2 (1803), 457. Thirty years later Southey rectified the problem by writing his own life of Cowper.

[13] *The Life of Nelson* (London: John Murray, 1813) 1:1. Subsequent references will be indicated in parentheses.

[14] *Letters and Journals of Lord Byron: With Notices of His Life* (London, 1830–31), 2:51.

[15] Hallam Tennyson, *Alfred Lord Tennyson, A Memoir By His Son* (London: Macmillan and Co., 1897), 1:xi.

[16] "Introduction" to *The Letters of Alfred Lord Tennyson*, ed. Cecil Y. Lang and Edgar F. Shannon, Jr. (Cambridge: Harvard University Press, 1981), xxix.

[17] Leslie Marchand, *Byron: A Biography* (New York: Alfred A. Knopf, 1957), 349, 977.

[18] *Memoirs of the Life of Sir Walter Scott, Bart.* (Edinburgh, 1837–38), 4:150. Subsequent references will be indicated in parentheses.

[19] See, for example, Davidson Cook, "Lockhart's Treatment of Scott's Letters," *Nineteenth Century* 102 (1927), 391–96; and Herbert Grierson, *Sir Walter Scott, Bart.* (New York: Columbia University Press, 1938), *passim*.

[20] Quoted in Francis R. Hart, *Lockhart as Romantic Biographer* (Edinburgh: Edinburgh University Press, 1971), p. 174n.

[21] Hart, p. 42.

[22] "Richter," *Edinburgh Review* 46 (1827), 177.

Chapter 2

[1] *Orlando* (New York: Harcourt Brace Jovanovich, 1956), 209.

[2] Letter to George and Georgiana Keats, 14 February–3 May 1819. H. E. Rollins, ed., *The Letters of John Keats* (Cambridge: Harvard University Press, 1958), 2:67. Subsequent references to the letters will be from this edition, identified by recipient and date in parentheses. Keats's erratic spelling and punctuation, which reflect the spontaneity of the writing, will be retained.

[3] *Life, Letters, and Literary Remains of John Keats* (London: Edward Moxon, 1848), 1:245.

[4] *Letters of John Keats to His Family and Friends* (London: Macmillan and Co., 1891), xiv, xvii.

[5] *John Keats* (Boston: Houghton Mifflin Co., 1925), *passim*.

[6] *The Use of Poetry and the Use of Criticism* (Cambridge: Harvard University Press, 1933), 91–92.

[7] *The Letters of John Keats*, 1:8–14.

[8] *The Letters of John Keats*, 1:20–23.

[9] Walter Jackson Bate, *John Keats* (Cambridge: Harvard University Press, 1963), 319.

[10] *The Prose Works of William Wordsworth*, ed. W. J. B. Owen and Jane Worthington Smyser (Oxford: Clarendon Press, 1974), 3:122.

[11] "To George Felton Mathew," Jack Stillinger, ed., *The Poems of John Keats* (Cambridge: Harvard University Press, 1978), line 9. Subsequent references to the poems of Keats are from this edition and will be cited with line numbers in parentheses.

[12] See, for example, Claude Lee Finney, *The Evolution of Keats's Poetry* (Cambridge:

Harvard University Press, 1936), 1:209–322; and J. D. Wigod, "The Meaning of *Endymion*," *PMLA* 68 (September 1953), 779–90.

[13] Bate, 169.

[14] *John Keats: The Living Year* (Cambridge: Harvard University Press, 1954).

[15] Gittings, 54–63; Murry, *Keats* (London: Jonathan Cape, 1955), 130–44.

[16] *Victoria Magazine* (May 1870), 55–67.

[17] Edmund Blunden, *Keats's Publisher* (London: Jonathan Cape, 1936), 89.

[18] Dorothy Hyde Bodurtha and Willard Bissell Pope, "Introduction" to *Life of John Keats By Charles Armitage Brown* (London: Oxford University Press, 1937), pp. 4–9.

[19] In G. M. Matthews, ed., *Keats: The Critical Heritage* (London: Routledge and Kegan Paul, 1971), 249–55.

[20] In Matthews, pp. 261–63.

Chapter 3

[1] *The Letters of Charles Armitage Brown*, ed. Jack Stillinger (Cambridge: Harvard University Press, 1966), 415. Subsequent references will be identified by recipient and date in parentheses.

[2] James Pope-Hennessy, *Monckton Milnes* (London: Constable, 1949), 1:22.

[3] *The Education of Henry Adams* (New York: Modern Library, 1931), 139.

[4] *The Romantic Agony* (London: Oxford University Press, 1951), 215–16.

[5] Unsigned review, "Monckton Milnes," *Times Literary Supplement* (17 February 1959), 98.

[6] *The Keats Circle* (Cambridge: Harvard University Press, 1948), vol. 2, *passim*. See also the "Introduction" to Charles Brown's *Life of Keats*, ed. Dorothy Hyde Bodurtha and Willard Bissell Pope (London: Oxford University Press, 1937) for details on the various early projects for a memoir of Keats.

[7] *Lord Byron and Some of His Contemporaries* (London: Henry Colburn, 1828), 1:439. Subsequent references from this volume will be indicated in parentheses.

[8] W. J. Bate, *John Keats* (Cambridge: Harvard University Press, 1963), 614–16. See also Sir William Hale-White, *Keats as Doctor and Patient* (London: Oxford University Press, 1938), pp. 43–51.

[9] *The Keats Circle*, 2:96.

[10] Bodurtha and Pope, "Introduction," 35.

[11] It seems, in fact, that Milnes helped to preserve Brown's image in this controversy. Brown had already gone to Scotland for the summer, as was his custom, when he received Keats's request for his company on the journey to Italy. Returning to London, he found that he had missed Keats's boat by hours, and wrote in the "Life" that he resolved "to follow him very early in the spring." By "very early in the spring" Keats was already dead; Milnes thoughtfully paraphrased Brown's resolution to read "following Keats as speedily as possible." See Milnes's *Life, Letters and Literary Remains of John Keats* (London: Edward Moxon, 1848), II, 71. Subsequent references will be indicated in parentheses.

[12] "The New Biography," in *Granite and Rainbow* (London: Hogarth Press, 1958), 151.

[13] "Preface" to *Eminent Victorians* (London: Chatto and Windus, 1918), viii.

[14] *Lives of the English Poets*, ed. George Birkbeck Hill (Oxford: Clarendon Press, 1905), 3:297–98.

[15] See *Newsweek* (26 December 1966) on the controversy surrounding William Manchester's publication of intimate material in his *The Death of a President*, on John F. Kennedy.

More recently, Edward Mendelson and Stephen Spender decided to delay the publication of an authorized biography of W. H. Auden as long as those who might be wounded by its disclosures are still alive. See Mendelson's "Authorized Biography and Its Discontents," in *Studies in Biography*, ed. Daniel Aaron (Cambridge: Harvard University Press, 1978), 9–26.

[16] *Truth to Life: The Art of Biography in the Nineteenth Century* (New York: Harcourt Brace Jovanovich, 1974), p. 32.

[17] *Memoirs of the Life of Sir Walter Scott, Bart.* (Edinburgh, 1837–38), 5:137.

[18] *Blackwood's Magazine* 23 (March 1828), 396–97.

[19] *Lives and Letters* (New York: Alfred A. Knopf, 1965), 82–88.

[20] John Morley, "A New Calendar of Great Men," *Nineteenth Century* 31 (1892), 312–28.

[21] Printed in William Holman Hunt's *Pre-Raphaelitism and the Pre-Raphaelite Brotherhood* (London, 1914), 1:111.

[22] *The Keats Circle*, 2:54.

[23] *Literary Essays* (Boston, 1892), 1:219–20.

[24] *The Poetical Works of John Keats* (London: Edward Moxon, 1856), xii.

[25] "Introduction," *The Poetical Works of John Keats* (London: E. Moxon, Son, & Co., 1872), ix.

[26] Quoted in a review by Benjamin DeMott, *New York Times Book Review* 87 (31 October 1982), 12.

[27] Altick cites these examples, 172–73.

[28] Quoted in Howard Mumford Jones, *The Harp That Once—* (New York: H. Holt & Co., 1937), 352.

[29] Hill, 2:116.

[30] Margaret Lane, "Introduction," *Charlotte Brontë*, by Elizabeth Gaskell (London: John Lehman, 1947), ix–x.

[31] *The Idea of a University* (New York: Longmans, Green, and Co., 1927), 209.

[32] "Modern Biography," *Blackwood's Edinburgh Magazine* 65 (February 1849), 222.

[33] *The Keats Circle*, 2:159, 131.

[34] Edwin G. Wilson, "Edward Moxon and the First Two Editions of Milnes's Biography of Keats," *Harvard Library Bulletin* V (Winter 1951), 125–29.

[35] T. Wemyss Reid, *The Life, Letters, and Friendships of Richard Monckton Milnes, First Lord Houghton* (London: Cassell and Company, 1890), 1:201.

[36] *The Diary of Benjamin Robert Haydon*, ed. Willard Bissell Pope (Cambridge: Harvard University Press, 1960), 2:318; *The Keats Circle*, 2:274.

Chapter 4

[1] *Keats and the Victorians* (New Haven: Yale University Press, 1944), 68.

[2] J. R. MacGillivray, *Keats: A Bibliography and Reference Guide* (Toronto: University of Toronto Press, 1949), liv.

[3] "Memoir," *The Poetical Works of John Keats* (London: George Bell and Sons, 1876), xxiii. Subsequent references will be included in parentheses in the text.

[4] *Dante Gabriel Rossetti: His Family Letters*, ed. William Michael Rossetti (Boston: Roberts Brothers, 1895), 2:39.

[5] T. Hall Caine, *Recollections of Dante Gabriel Rossetti* (London: Elliot Stock, 1882), 167. It should be noted that Rossetti's enthusiasms, like those of Landor and Swinburne, were sometimes extravagant. He also called *The Princess* "the finest poem since Shakespeare."

[6] Caine, *Recollections of Rossetti*: (London: Cassell and Co., 1928), 120.

⁷ *John Keats: Criticism and Comment* (London: Richard Clay and Sons, for private circulation, 1919), p. 12. This pamphlet consists of five letters written to Harry Buxton Forman in 1881.

⁸ Chatterton also fascinated the French, usually—as with Byron and Poe—for superficial, if not downright misguided, reasons. Alfred de Vigny's play *Chatterton* contains no notion of the kind of poetry his hero wrote; it is simply a lament against the crass society that makes martyrs of its poets. In many cases, the image counts for more than the substance.

⁹ "Memoir," *The Poetical Works of John Keats* (London: Edward Moxon, 1856), xlvi–xlvii.

¹⁰ See the letters to Reynolds (21 September 1819) and to George and Georgiana (24 September 1819), and *The Keats Circle*, 2:276.

¹¹ "Five English Poets," *Rossetti's Poems*, ed. Oswald Doughty (London: J. M. Dent, 1968), 252–54.

¹² Caine, 189, 190.

¹³ Of course, some opponents of Philistine criticism remained unconvinced. Hall Caine, for instance, still believed in 1882 that criticism "did more than all else" to end Keats's life (176).

¹⁴ (New York: Farrar, Straus, and Giroux, 1977), 11–20.

¹⁵ Sontag, 18.

¹⁶ Quoted in Sontag, 29.

¹⁷ Quoted in Sontag, 31.

¹⁸ Sontag, 20.

¹⁹ *Life, Letters, and Literary Remains of John Keats* (London: Edward Moxon, 1848), 2:66.

²⁰ In G. M. Matthews, *Keats: The Critical Heritage* (London: Routledge & Kegan Paul, 1971), 306.

²¹ *Life, Letters, and Literary Remains*, 2:108.

²² Caine, 169.

²³ "Maurice de Guérin," *Essays in Criticism*, First Series (London: Macmillan and Co., 1865), 109.

²⁴ *Letters of John Keats to Fanny Brawne* (London: Reeves and Turner, 1878), xvi.

²⁵ "Our Library Table," *The Athenaeum* No. 2625 (16 February 1878), 218.

²⁶ "An Improbable Life," a review of the letters of Oscar Wilde, *New Yorker* 39 (9 March 1963), 155–177. Auden assumes essentially the same position taken by Wordsworth in his "Letter to a Friend of Robert Burns": "Since knowledge of an artist's private life never throws any significant light upon his work, there is no justification for intruding upon his privacy."

²⁷ In Georges Lafourcade, *Swinburne's Hyperion and other Poems* (London: Faber and Gwyer, 1927), 31–32.

²⁸ Lafourcade, 31–40.

²⁹ Ford, pp. 165–67; Lafourcade, *passim*.

³⁰ *A Midsummer Holiday And Other Poems* (London: Chatto and Windus, 1884), pp. 134–38.

³¹ Of course, they were not alone. Dreading the controversy stirred by publication of letters like those of Keats and the Carlyles, writers from Dickens to Hardy took pains to burn as many of their letters as possible. Wordsworth also had a plan for maintaining his privacy: he claimed that the reason his letters were so dull was a strategy to ensure their being discarded. See Altick, *Lives and Letters*, 161.

³² "John Keats," *Encyclopedia Britannica* (Cambridge: Cambridge University Press, 1911), 11th ed., 15:708. The following quotations of Swinburne are from this reprint of his 1882 essay.

³³ Ford, 169. See also Mario Praz, *The Romantic Agony* (London: Oxford University Press, 1951), 239, where Praz holds Swinburne's judgment of Keats's letters in the lurid light of Swinburne's own sexual inclinations.

34 *The Letters of Matthew Arnold to Arthur Hugh Clough*, ed. Howard Foster Lowry (London: Oxford University Press, 1932), 96.

35 "Table-Talk," *The Complete Works of William Hazlitt*, ed. P. P. Howe (London: J. M. Dent, 1930–34), 8:254.

36 "Le Paganisme poétique en Angleterre," *Revue des Deux Mondes* 69 (15 May 1867), 298.

37 "John Keats," *Essays in Criticism*, 2d ser. (London: Macmillan and Co., 1902), 103. Subsequent references to this text will be indicated with page numbers in parentheses.

38 *The Diary of Benjamin Robert Haydon*, ed. Willard B. Pope (Cambridge: Harvard University Press, 1960), 2:317.

39 W. J. Bate, *John Keats* (Cambridge, Harvard University Press, 1963), 463–64n.

40 Lowry, 139.

41 "The Life of Keats," prefixed to *The Poetical Works of John Keats* (Boston, 1854), xv.

42 As Ford shows (74–89), "The Scholar Gipsy" and "Thyrsis" especially bear the Keatsian stamp.

CHAPTER 5

1 For more extensive treatment of the development of biography, see Richard Altick, *Lives and Letters* (New York: Alfred A. Knopf, 1965) and A. O. J. Cockshut, *Truth to Life* (New York: Harcourt Brace Jovanovich, 1974).

2 "Biography," *Critical and Miscellaneous Essays* (London: Chapman and Hall, 1899), 3:44–61; *The Life of John Sterling* (London: Chapman and Hall, 1897).

3 E. V. Lucas, *The Colvins and Their Friends* (London: Methuen & Co., 1928), p. 134.

4 Altick, *Victorian People and Ideas* (New York: W. W. Norton & Co., 1973), 299–304.

5 *National Review* 22 (September 1893), 181.

6 Those who desire an interesting detour, however, will find it in Waldo Dunn's *Froude and Carlyle* (London: Longman's, Green and Co., 1930).

7 We cannot be sure that "The Dead Prophet" is specifically about Carlyle, just as we are not certain that "To ———, After Reading A Life And Letters" was provoked by Milnes's *Life* of Keats. But the circumstantial evidence seems strong for both. In spite of the mysterious subtitle "182—," an earlier draft of "The Dead Prophet" apparently dates from the early 'eighties, and we know from Tennyson's *Memoir* that he disliked Froude's *Carlyle*. See Jerome Hamilton Buckley, *Tennyson: The Growth of a Poet* (Cambridge: Harvard University Press, 1960), 284.

8 *Life of John Keats* (London: Walter Scott, 1887), 9. Subsequent references will be indicated with page numbers in parentheses.

9 *The Poetical Works of John Keats* (London: E. Moxon, Son, & Co., 1872), p. ix *n*. Subsequent references will be indicated with page numbers in parentheses.

10 "Recollections of Keats," *Atlantic Monthly*, January 1861, 86–100.

11 *John Keats* (London: Heinemann, 1968), 446–50.

12 *The Letters of Robert Louis Stevenson*, ed. Colvin (New York: Charles Scribner's Sons, 1911), 1:xv. Subsequent references will be indicated with page numbers in parentheses.

13 Delancey Ferguson and Marshall Waingrow, eds., *Stevenson's Letters to Charles Baxter* (New Haven: Yale University Press, 1956), xvii.

14 Richard Aldington, *Portrait of a Rebel: The Life and Work of Robert Louis Stevenson* (London: Evans Brothers Limited, 1957), p. 227. In fairness to Colvin, it should be noted that the Stevenson of his edition is not so egregiously falsified as the hero of the authorized biography by Stevenson's cousin Graham Balfour—the "Seraph in Chocolate" that Henley refused to recognize in his *Pall Mall* review.

¹⁵ *Letters of John Keats to His Family and Friends* (London: Macmillan and Co., 1891), xv–xvi.

¹⁶ *Keats* (London: Macmillan and Co., 1887), vi. Subsequent references will be indicated with page numbers in parentheses.

¹⁷ Gittings, 451.

¹⁸ "On the Vicissitudes of Keats's Fame," *Atlantic Monthly*, April 1863, 401–7.

¹⁹ The best-known statement of the critical use of biography is Browning's prefatory essay to a volume of Shelley's letters. "In our approach to poetry," he wrote, "we necessarily approach the personality of the poet; in apprehending it we apprehend him, and certainly we cannot love it without loving him. Both for love's and for understanding's sake we desire to know him, and, as readers of his poetry, must be readers of his biography also." Later, of course, Browning recanted fiercely, especially in the poem "House" (1876). See Altick, *Lives and Letters*, 95–98, 158–59.

²⁰ *Life, Letters, and Literary Remains of John Keats* (London: Edward Moxon, 1848), 1:11.

²¹ *Quarterly Review* No. 332 (April 1888), 311.

²² "Keats's Place in English Poetry," *National Review* 10 (September 1887), 21.

²³ "Critical Introduction," *Poems of John Keats*, ed. G. Thorn Drury (London: Lawrence and Bullen, 1896), 1:xcvii, cv.

²⁴ *John Keats* (Boston: Houghton Mifflin, 1908), vii. Subsequent references will be indicated with page numbers in parentheses.

²⁵ The process of emendation started immediately. Louis Arthur Holman, an American collector of Keatsiana, noted "seventy-odd 'slips of the pen' " in Colvin's 1917 volume, and published them in the *Boston Evening Transcript* (3 July 1918). In Colvin's third edition (1920) seven of nineteen substantive errors had been corrected, by Holman's count. Holman's annotated copy of Colvin, which contains this information, is now in the Keats Collection of the Houghton Library at Harvard.

CHAPTER 6

¹ "Thomas Carlyle," in *Biographical Essays* (New York: Harcourt, Brace and World, 1969), 255.

² "A Statesman: Lord Morley," in *Characters and Commentaries*, ed. James Strachey (New York: Harcourt, Brace and Co., 1933), 215.

³ *Eminent Victorians* (London: Chatto and Windus, 1918), viii. Subsequent references will be indicated with page numbers in parentheses.

⁴ One of the best-known novelistic biographies is André Maurois' *Ariel* (1923), which frankly calls itself "A Shelley Romance." It is a web of overheard thoughts and invented scenes. Strachey's copy, now in the Houghton Library at Harvard, is inscribed by the author "À M. Lytton Strachey grand peintre de portraits cette pâle esquisse est dediée en très vive admiration."

⁵ *Shelley* (New York: Alfred A. Knopf, 1940), 1:vii.

⁶ "The New Biography," in *Granite and Rainbow* (London: Hogarth Press, 1958), 150.

⁷ Richard Altick, *Lives and Letters* (New York: Alfred A. Knopf, 1965), 292.

⁸ "Lytton Strachey and the Art of Biography," *Memories* (New York: Oxford University Press, 1953), 39, 32.

⁹ *The Art of the Novel: Critical Prefaces* (New York: Charles Scribner's Sons, 1934), xvi.

¹⁰ Letter of 25 July 1922, in Hyder Edward Rollins and Stephen Maxfield Parrish, *Keats and the Bostonians* (Cambridge: Harvard University Press, 1951), 136. Subsequent references will be indicated in parentheses as *Bostonians*, with page numbers.

[11] S. Foster Damon, *Amy Lowell: A Chronicle* (Boston: Houghton Mifflin Co., 1935), 98–107.

[12] *John Keats* (Boston: Houghton Mifflin Co. 1925), 1:33. Subsequent references will be indicated with page numbers in parentheses.

[13] Edmund Gosse, whose stylized autobiography *Father and Son* (1907) anticipated Strachey's work in its rhetorical manipulation and its attitude towards an eminent Victorian (his father), announced the modern opposition to biographical evasiveness most vociferously. The biographer's task, he declared in "The Ethics of Biography" (*Cosmopolitan* 35 [July 1903], 317), is "to be as indiscreet as possible within the bounds of good taste and kind feeling." Unhappily for Gosse, one of his own major efforts in biography, a life of Swinburne (1917), was thoroughly bowdlerized because of the demands of his subject's family. See Altick, *Lives and Letters*, 246.

[14] Damon, 431. An example of the dangers of psychological criticism may be found in the appendix of a dissertation by Harold E. Briggs, the core of which is a useful edition of Milnes's *Life of Keats* (University of Minnesota, 1943, unpublished). Briggs discovers that Keats was "psychasthenic," "cyclothymic," and "autistic," proving in the process how unhelpful clinical terms are outside the clinic. Accepting Lowell's thesis that Keats was always in search of a mother, and pondering the lack of reference to his father in the letters, Briggs speculates that Keats's father beat him, and goes on to explain that Keats's agnosticism was the natural result: in excluding God from his system of salvation, Keats was expressing old repressed desires against his physical father. This is psychologizing, not psychology, and we should keep in mind Howard Mumford Jones's warning about its usefulness: "Since psychoanalysis depends upon the uncovering of submerged memories through free association under skillful guidance, it seems fair to remark that a dead author has neither memories nor associations nor the capability to be cross-examined" (quoted in Altick, 340).

[15] *The Complete Works of William Hazlitt*, ed. P. P. Howe (London: J. M. Dent and Sons, 1930–34), 1:2.

[16] *Rambler* No. 60, in *Selected Essays from the "Rambler," "Adventurer," and "Idler,"* ed. W. J. Bate (New Haven: Yale University, 1968), 109.

[17] *Selected Poetry and Prose of Shelley*, ed. Carlos Baker (New York: Modern Library, 1951), 502.

[18] Clement Wood, *Amy Lowell* (New York, 1926), 128.

[19] W. J. Bate, *John Keats* (Cambridge, Mass.: Harvard University Press, 1963), pp. 614–16.

[20] "John Keats," *The Dial* 78 (June 1925), 476.

[21] Quoted in Willard M. Gaylin, "Psychoanaliterature," *Columbia University Forum* 6 (Spring 1963), 14.

[22] Damon, 607–8.

[23] Damon, 657.

[24] See, for example, Samuel Chew, "Miss Lowell's Biography of Keats," *North American Review* 221 (March 1925), 545–55.

[25] "A Keats from America," *Sunday Times* (15 March 1925), 8.

[26] Clement Shorter, "A Literary Letter," *Sphere* (30 May 1925), p. 266. Later in the year Shorter noted in *Sphere* for August 8 (p. 164), "American editors are still animatedly discussing [my] assertion that Miss Amy Lowell died broken-hearted because Sir Edmund Gosse reviewed her biography of Keats unfavorably. The editor of the *Chicago Daily News* book-page observes: 'No, it is not likely that a review by Gosse killed Amy Lowell, but it is pretty certain that had Miss Lowell lived the review would have killed Gosse. Very likely it was this review that made her pack her trunk and announce that she was going to England. It would have been a delight to encounter her there, sitting opposite Sir Edmund and on J. C. Squire. It is easy to forecast who would pass out in that mêlée.' "

[27] *Memories and Studies* (New York: Longmans, Green, & Co., 1912), 322.

Epilogue

[1] *John Keats* (Cambridge: Harvard University Press, 1963), 2.
[2] *John Keats: The Making of a Poet* (New York: Viking Press, 1963), 44. Subsequent references will be indicated in parentheses.
[3] Bate, 132.
[4] Bate, 147.
[5] See above, 58.
[6] *The Listener* 71 (30 January 1964), 203.
[7] *John Keats* (London: Heinemann, 1968), v.
[8] Review article, *The Keats-Shelley Journal* 18 (1969), 107.

Bibliography

Adams, Henry. *The Education of Henry Adams.* New York: Modern Library, 1931.
Aiken, Conrad. "John Keats." *The Dial,* 78 (June 1925), 475-90.
Aldington, Richard. *The Portrait of a Rebel: The Life and Work of Robert Louis Stevenson.* London: Evans Brothers, 1957.
Altick, Richard D. *Lives and Letters: A History of Literary Biography in England and America.* New York: Alfred A. Knopf, 1965.
———. *Victorian People and Ideas.* New York: W. W. Norton & Co., 1973.
Arnold, Matthew. "John Keats." In *Essays in Criticism.* 2d ser. London: Macmillan and Co., Ltd., 1902.
———. *The Letters of Matthew Arnold to Arthur Hugh Clough.* Ed. Howard Foster Lowry. London: Oxford University Press, 1932.
———. "Maurice de Guérin." In *Essays in Criticism.* 1st ser. London: Macmillan and Co., 1865.
Auden, W. H. "An Improbable Life." *New Yorker* 39 (9 March 1963), 155-77.
Bate, Walter Jackson. *John Keats.* Cambridge, Mass.: Harvard University Press, 1963.
———. *The Stylistic Development of Keats.* Cambridge: Harvard University Press, 1945.
Blunden, Edmund. *Keats's Publisher.* London: Jonathan Cape, 1936.
Bridges, Robert. "Critical Introduction." In *Poems of John Keats.* 2 vols. Ed. G. Thorn Drury. New York: Charles Scribner's Sons, 1896.
Briggs, Harold E. "The First Life of Keats." Ph.D. diss., University of Minnesota, 1943.
Brown, Charles. *The Letters of Charles Armitage Brown.* Ed. Jack Stillinger, Cambridge: Harvard University Press, 1966.
———. *Life of John Keats.* Ed. Dorothy Hyde Bodurtha and Willard Bissell Pope. London: Oxford University Press, 1937.
Buckley, Jerome Hamilton. *Tennyson: The Growth of a Poet.* Cambridge: Harvard University Press, 1960.
Caine, T. Hall. *Recollections of Dante Gabriel Rossetti.* London: Elliot Stock, 1882.
Carlyle, Thomas. *Critical and Miscellaneous Essays.* 6 vols. London: Chapman and Hall, 1899.
———. *The Life of John Sterling.* 1851; rpt. London: Chapman and Hall, 1897.
———. "Richter." *Edinburgh Review,* 46 (1827), 176-95.
Chew, Samuel C. "Miss Lowell's Biography of Keats." *North American Review,* 221 (March 1925), 545-55.

Clarke, Charles Cowden. "Recollections of Keats." *Atlantic Monthly*, January 1861, pp. 86-100.
Clifford, James L. "How Much Should a Biographer Tell? Some Eighteenth-Century Views." In *Essays in Eighteenth-Century Biography*. Ed. Philip B. Daghlian. Bloomington, Ind.: University of Indiana Press, 1968, pp. 67-95.
_____. "Introduction." *Twentieth-Century Interpretations of Boswell's "Life of Johnson."* Englewood Cliffs, N.J.: Prentice-Hall, 1970.
Cockshut, A. O. J. *Truth to Life: The Art of Biography in the Nineteenth Century*. New York: Harcourt Brace Jovanovich, 1974.
Colvin, Sidney. *John Keats: His Life and Poetry: His Friends, Critics, and After-Fame*. 1917; rpt. New York: Charles Scribner's Sons, 1925.
_____. *Keats*. New York: Harper and Brothers, 1887.
Cook, Davidson. "Lockhart's Treatment of Scott's Letters." *Nineteenth Century* 102 (1927), 391-96.
Courthope, William John. "Keats's Place in English Poetry." *The National Review*, 10 (September 1887), 11-24.
"The Daintiest of Poets." *Victoria Magazine* (May 1870), pp. 55-67.
Damon, S. Foster, *Amy Lowell: A Chronicle*. Boston: Houghton Mifflin Co., 1935.
DeMott, Benjamin. "Intelligence at Work." *New York Times Book Review* 87 (31 October 1982), 12.
Dilke, Charles Wentworth. "Our Library Table." *The Athenaeum* No. 2625 (16 February 1878), 218.
Dunn, Waldo. *Froude and Carlyle*. London: Longmans, Green and Co., 1930.
Edel, Leon. *Literary Biography*. Bloomington, Indiana: Indiana University Press, 1959.
Eliot, T. S. *The Use of Poetry and the Use of Criticism*. Cambridge: Harvard University Press, 1933.
Ellman, Richard. *Yeats: The Man and the Masks*. London: Macmillan and Co., 1949.
Étienne, Louis. "Le Paganisme poétique en Angleterre." *La Revue des Deux Mondes* 69 (15 May 1867), 291-317.
Finney, Claude Lee. *The Evolution of Keats's Poetry*. 2 vols. Cambridge: Harvard University Press, 1936.
Ford, George. *Keats and the Victorians*. New Haven: Yale University Press, 1944.
Froude, James Anthony. *Thomas Carlyle*. 4 vols. New York: Charles Scribner's Sons, 1882-84.
Gaskell, Elizabeth. *The Life of Charlotte Brontë*. Ed. Clement K. Shorter. New York: Harper and Brothers, 1900.
Gaylin, Willard M. "Psychoanaliterature: The Hazards of a Hybrid." *Columbia University Forum* 6 (Spring 1963), 11-16.
Gittings, Robert. *John Keats*. London: Heinemann, 1968.
_____. *John Keats: The Living Year*. Cambridge: Harvard University Press, 1954.
_____. Review of *John Keats*, by W. J. Bate. *The Listener* 71 (January 1964), 203-4.
Gosse, Edmund. "The Ethics of Biography." *Cosmopolitan* 35 (July 1903), 317-23.
_____. "A Keats from America." *Sunday Times* (15 March 1925), 8.
Grierson, Herbert. *Sir Walter Scott, Bart*. New York: Columbia University Press, 1938.
Hale-White, William. *Keats as Doctor and Patient*. London: Oxford University Press, 1938.
Hancock, Albert Elmer. *John Keats*. Boston: Houghton Mifflin Co., 1908.
Hart, Francis R. "Boswell and the Romantics: A Chapter in the History of Biographical Theory." *ELH* 27 (March 1960), 44-65.
_____. *Lockhart as Romantic Biographer*. Edinburgh: Edinburgh University Press, 1971.
_____. "Proofreading Lockhart's *Scott*: The Dynamics of Biographical Reticence." *Studies in Bibliography* 14 (1961), 3-22.

Haydon, Benjamin Robert. *Autobiography.* 2 vols. London: Peter Davies, 1926.
_____. *The Diary of Benjamin Robert Haydon.* 5 vols. Ed. Willard B. Pope. Cambridge: Harvard University Press, 1960.
Hazlitt, William. *The Complete Works of William Hazlitt.* 21 vols. Ed. P. P. Howe. London: J. M. Dent, 1931.
Hunt, Leigh. *Lord Byron and Some of His Contemporaries.* 2 vols. London: Henry Colburn, 1828.
Hunt, William Holman. *Pre-Raphaelitism and the Pre-Raphaelite Brotherhood.* 2 vols. London: Macmillan and Co., 1914.
Jack, Ian. "Two Biographers: Lockhart and Boswell." In *Johnson, Boswell and Their Circle.* Oxford: Clarendon Press, 1965, pp. 268-85.
James, Henry. *The Art of the Novel: Critical Prefaces.* New York: Charles Scribner's Sons, 1934.
James, William. *Memories and Studies.* New York: Longmans, Green, & Co., 1912.
Johnson, Samuel. *Lives of the English Poets.* 3 vols. Ed. George Birkbeck Hill. Oxford: Clarendon Press, 1905.
_____. *Selected Essays from the "Rambler," "Adventurer," and "Idler."* Ed. W. J. Bate. New Haven: Yale University Press, 1968.
Jones, Howard Mumford. *The Harp That Once—: A Chronicle of the Life of Thomas Moore.* New York: H. Holt & Co., 1937.
Keats, John. *The Letters of John Keats, 1814-1821.* 2 vols. Ed. Hyder Edward Rollins. Cambridge: Harvard University Press, 1958.
_____. *Letters of John Keats to Fanny Brawne.* Ed. Harry Buxton Forman. London: Reeves and Turner, 1878.
_____. *Letters of John Keats to His Family and Friends.* Ed. Sidney Colvin. London: Macmillan and Co., 1891.
_____. *The Poems of John Keats.* Ed. Jack Stillinger. Cambridge: Harvard University Press, 1978.
Lafourcade, Georges. *Swinburne's Hyperion and Other Poems.* London: Faber and Gwyer, 1927.
Lane, Margaret. "Introduction." *Charlotte Brontë.* By Elizabeth Gaskell. London: John Lehman, 1947.
Lockhart, John Gibson. *Memoirs of the Life of Sir Walter Scott, Bart.* 7 vols. Edinburgh: Robert Cadell, 1837-38.
Lowell, Amy. *John Keats.* 2 vols. Boston: Houghton Mifflin Co., 1925.
Lowell, James Russell. "The Life of Keats." In *The Poetical Works of John Keats.* Boston: n.p., 1854.
_____. *Literary Essays.* 4 vols. Boston: Houghton Mifflin Co., 1892.
Lucas, E. V. *The Colvins and Their Friends.* London: Methuen and Co., Ltd., 1928
Lyons, John O. *The Invention of the Self: The Hinge of Consciousness in the Eighteenth Century.* Carbondale, Illinois: Southern Illinois University Press, 1978.
MacCarthy, Desmond. "Lytton Strachey and the Art of Biography." In *Memories.* New York: Oxford University Press, 1953.
MacGillivray, J. R. *Keats: A Bibliography and Reference Guide.* Toronto: University of Toronto Press, 1949.
Marchand, Leslie. *Byron: A Biography.* 3 vols. New York: Alfred A. Knopf, 1957.
Masefield, John. *Poems.* New York: Macmillan, 1960.
Matthews, G. M., ed. *Keats: The Critical Heritage.* London: Routledge & Kegan Paul, 1971.
Maurois, André. *Ariel, ou la vie de Shelley.* Paris: Bernard Grasset, 1923.
Mendelson, Edward. "Authorized Biography and Its Discontents." In *Studies in Biography.* Ed. Daniel Aaron, Cambridge: Harvard University Press, 1978, 9-26.

Milnes, Richard Monckton (Lord Houghton). *Life, Letters, and Literary Remains of John Keats.* 2 vols. London: Edward Moxon, 1848.

———. "Memoir." *The Poetical Works of John Keats.* London: Edward Moxon, 1856.

———. "Memoir." *The Poetical Works of John Keats.* London: George Bell and Sons, 1876.

"Modern Biography." *Blackwood's Edinburgh Magazine* 65 (February 1849), 219–34.

"Monckton Milnes." *Times Literary Supplement* (17 February 1959), pp. 97–98.

Moore, Doris Langley. *The Late Lord Byron.* London: John Murray, 1961.

Moore, Thomas. *Letters and Journals of Lord Byron: With Notices of His Life.* 2 vols. London: John Murray, 1830–31.

———. "The 'Living Dog' and the 'Dead Lion.'" *Blackwood's Magazine* 23 (March 1828), 396–97.

Morley, John. *Burke.* London: Harper and Brothers, 1878.

———. "A New Calendar of Great Men." *Nineteenth Century* 31 (1892), 312–28.

Murry, John Middleton. *Keats.* London: Jonathan Cape, 1955.

Newman, John Henry. *The Idea of a University.* New York: Longmans, Green, and Co., 1927.

Pope-Hennessy, James. *Monckton Milnes.* 2 vols. London: Constable, 1949.

Praz, Mario. *The Romantic Agony.* London: Oxford University Press, 1951.

Prothero, R. N. Review of biographies by Colvin and W. M. Rossetti. *Quarterly Review* No. 332 (April 1888), 308–38.

Reed, Joseph W., Jr. *English Biography in the Early Nineteenth Century.* New Haven: Yale University Press, 1966.

Reid, T. Wemyss. *The Life, Letters, and Friendships of Richard Monckton Milnes, First Lord Houghton.* 2 vols. London: Cassell and Company, 1890.

Rollins, Hyder Edward, and Stephen Maxfield Parrish. *Keats and the Bostonians.* Cambridge: Harvard University Press, 1951.

Rollins, Hyder Edward, ed. *The Keats Circle.* 2 vols. Cambridge: Harvard University Press, 1948.

Rossetti, Dante Gabriel. *Dante Gabriel Rossetti: His Family Letters.* 2 vols. Ed. William Michael Rossetti. Boston: Roberts Brothers, 1895.

———. *John Keats: Criticism and Comment.* London: Richard Clay and Sons, 1919.

———. *Rossetti's Poems.* Ed. Oswald Doughty. London: J. M. Dent, 1968.

Rossetti, William Michael. "Introduction." *The Poetical Works of John Keats.* London: E. Moxon, Son, & Co., 1872.

———. *Life of John Keats.* London: Walter Scott, 1887.

———. *Lives of Famous Poets.* London: E. Moxon, Son & Co., 1878.

———. "Memoir." In *The Poetical Works of John Keats.* London: E. Moxon, Son, & Co., 1872.

Severn, Joseph. "On the Vicissitudes of Keats's Fame." *Atlantic Monthly,* April 1863, 401–7.

Sharp, William. *The Life and Letters of Joseph Severn.* London: Sampson Low, Marston & Company, 1892.

Shelley, Percy Bysshe. *Selected Poetry and Prose of Shelley.* Ed. Carlos Baker. New York: Modern Library, 1951.

Shorter, Clement. "A Literary Letter." *The Sphere* (30 May 1925), 266.

———. "A Literary Letter." *The Sphere* (8 August 1925), 164.

Sontag, Susan. *Illness as Metaphor.* New York: Farrar, Straus, and Giroux, 1977.

Southey, Robert. *The Life of Nelson.* 2 vols. London: John Murray, 1813.

———. Review of William Hayley's *Life of Cowper. Annual Review* 2 (1803), 457–62.

Stephen, Leslie. "Biography." *National Review* 22 (1893), 171–83.

Stevenson, Robert Louis. *The Letters of Robert Louis Stevenson.* 4 vols. Ed. Sidney Colvin. New York: Charles Scribner's Sons, 1911.

———. *Stevenson's Letters to Charles Baxter.* Ed. Delancey Ferguson and Marshall Waingrow. New Haven: Yale University Press, 1956.

Stillinger, Jack. Review of *John Keats*, by Robert Gittings. *The Keats-Shelley Journal* 18 (1969), 107–11.

Strachey, Lytton. *Eminent Victorians.* London: Chatto & Windus, 1918.

———. "A Statesman: Lord Morley." In *Characters and Commentaries.* Ed James Strachey. New York: Harcourt, Brace and Company, 1933.

———. "Thomas Carlyle." In *Biographical Essays.* New York: Harcourt, Brace and World, 1969.

Swinburne, Algernon Charles. "John Keats." *Encyclopedia Britannica.* 11th ed. (1911), 15, 708–10.

———. *A Midsummer Holiday And Other Poems.* London: Chatto & Windus, 1884.

Tennyson, Alfred. *The Letters of Alfred Lord Tennyson.* Ed. Cecil Y. Lang and Edgar F. Shannon, Jr. Cambridge: Harvard University Press, 1981.

Tennyson, Hallam. *Alfred Lord Tennyson, A Memoir By His Son.* 2 vols. London: Macmillan and Co., 1897.

Trilling, Lionel. "Introduction." *The Selected Letters of John Keats.* Ed. Lionel Trilling. New York: Farrar, Straus and Young, 1951.

Weller, Earl V. *Autobiography of John Keats.* Stanford, California: Stanford University Press, 1933.

White, Newman Ivey. *Shelley.* 2 vols. New York: Alfred Knopf, 1940.

Wigod, J. D. "The Meaning of *Endymion.*" *PMLA* 68 (September 1953), 779–90.

Wilson, Edwin G. "Edward Moxon and the First Two Editions of Milnes's Biography of Keats." *Harvard Library Bulletin* 5 (Winter 1951), 125–29.

Wood, Clement. *Amy Lowell.* New York: Harold Vinal, 1926.

Woolf, Virginia. "The New Biography." In *Granite and Rainbow.* London: Hogarth Press, 1958.

———. *Orlando.* New York: Harcourt Brace Jovanovich, 1956.

Wordsworth, William. *The Prose Works of William Wordsworth.* Ed. W. J. B. Owen and Jane Worthington Smyser. Oxford: Clarendon Press, 1974.

Index

Abbey, Richard, 97, 98, 112
Adams, Henry, 38
Aesthetes, the, 61, 72–73
Aiken, Conrad, 105, 107
Altick, Richard D., 2, 46
Arnold, Matthew, 59, 61; early judgment of Keats, 69–70; response to Keats's love letters, 16, 24, 70–72; *Empedocles on Etna*, 69, 70
Auden, W. H., 66, 83

Bailey, Benjamin, 39, 44, 56, 60; Amy Lowell's view of, 102
Barrett, Elizabeth, 24
Bate, Walter Jackson, 27, 111–12, 113
Baxter, Charles, 83
Blake, William, 62–63, 64
Boswell, James, 5; *The Life of Johnson*, 6–9, 11, 12, 45–46
Brawne, Fanny, 18, 29, 30; John Keats's letters to, 16, 23–25, 66–67 (*see also* Arnold, Matthew; Colvin, Sidney; Lowell, Amy; Rossetti, Dante Gabriel; Rossetti, William Michael); letters to Fanny Keats, 87, 98, 106, 107; R. M. Milnes treatment of, 50–51, 64
Bridges, Robert, 88
Briggs, Harold E., 49, 122n.14
Brown, Charles, 34, 37; on Keats's origins, 47; "Life of John Keats," 17–18, 35, 38–40, 41–42, 60; Amy Lowell's view of, 102; on suppressing facts about Fanny Brawne, 50, 51
Browning, Robert, 24, 69, 76, 121n.19
Burns, Robert, 54, 67

Byron, George Gordon, Lord, 64; *Don Juan*, 40; as subject of biography, 10–12, 15, 45; view of Keats, 40, 41, 42, 56, 79

Caine, Hall, 119n.13
Carlyle, Thomas, 6, 14, 76, 78; "Heroes and Hero-Worship," 46; *The Life of Sterling*, 44, 76
Chatterton, Thomas, 62–63, 119n.8
Clarke, Charles Cowden, 34, 39, 80, 110
Clough, Arthur Hugh, 69
Cockshut, A. O. J., 45
Coleridge, Samuel Taylor, 1, 7, 18, 63; *Biographia Literaria*, 15
Colvin, Sidney, 3, 59, 109, 110; *Life of Keats* (1887), 75–76, 77, 78–79, 82–90, 106; Amy Lowell's opposition to, 96, 97, 98, 101, 105; view of Keats's letters to Fanny Brawne, 16, 85, 87, 90
Comte, Auguste, 46
Courthope, William John, 88
Cross, J. W., 48
Curll, Edmund, 6

Dante, 30
Day, Fred Holland, 97, 98, 106
Dickens, Charles, 11, 76, 119n.31
Dilke, Charles (Keats's friend), 50
Dilke, Charles Wentworth, Sir, 66, 106
Disraeli, Benjamin, 76; *Tancred*, 38
D'Israeli, Isaac, 7

Eliot, George (Mary Ann Evans), 48
Eliot, T. S., 16
Etienne, Louis, 70

Ford, George, 2, 59, 69
Forman, Harry Buxton, 85, 109; *Letters of John Keats to Fanny Brawne*, 16, 60, 66, 67–69, 70–72, 79–80. *See also* Arnold, Matthew; Brawne, Fanny; Rossetti, Dante Gabriel; Rossetti, William Michael; Swinburne, Algernon Charles
Freud, Sigmund, 76, 94, 98, 106, 110, 112
Froude, James Anthony, *Life of Carlyle*, 78, 83

Gaskell, Elizabeth, *Charlotte Brontë*, 50
Gautier, Théophile, 63–64
Gilfillan, George, 65
Gittings, Robert, 29, 81, 85, 112–13
Gosse, Edmund, 107, 122n.13, 122n.26

Hancock, Albert Elmer, 89
Hardy, Thomas, 11, 119n.31
Hart, Francis R., 13
Haslam, William, 39, 51
Haydon, Benjamin Robert, 19, 55, 56, 64, 81, 87, 104; *Autobiography*, 60, 71, 80; on Keats's drinking, 55, 71, 80; quarrel with Leigh Hunt, 33, 41, 49
Hayley, William, *Life of Cowper*, 9
Hazlitt, William, 19, 69–70, 100; *Essay on the Principles of Human Action*, 99
Henley, William Ernest, 82, 84
Holman, Louis, 96, 97, 121n.25
Hunt, Leigh, 19, 39, 66, 95, 96; Sidney Colvins's view of, 87; on Keats's illness, 38, 42; on Keats's origins, 47; *Lord Byron and Some of His Contemporaries*, 34–35, 38, 40–41, 45, 50; W. M. Rossetti's view of, 80
Hunt, William Holman, 61

James, Henry, 92, 95
James, William, 107
Jeffrey, John, 18
Johnson, Samuel: on biography, 1, 6, 34, 43, 49, 100, 116n.11; "Life of Addison," 49; "Life of Thomson," 43; *The Rambler*, 6; as subject of biography, 6–8
Jones, Isabella, 29, 113

Keats, Fanny, 87, 98, 106
Keats, George, 20, 22, 44, 88; suspected by Charles Brown, 35, 38, 102
Keats, John: aesthetic beliefs, 20–21; autobiography in the works of, 15–35; birth and background, 47–48; character revealed in works, 31–33; drinking and social life, 55; illness, 40–41, 63–66, 103–4; letters of, 11, 16–25; "negative capability," 19, 99; philosophical speculations, 21; poems as autobiography, 25–31; religious views, 33, 51–52, 86, 105; ribaldry, 54, 85–86, 105; romance with Fanny Brawne, 23–25, 50–51, 60, 63, 66–69, 70–72, 106; sense of humor, 21–23, 53–54, 80–81, 105
WORKS: "Dear Reynolds, as last night I lay in bed" ("Epistle to John Hamilton Reynolds"), 28; *Endymion*, 5, 25, 27–28, 29, 31, 41, 55, 60, 62, 68, 87, 88, 90, 97, 101, 102, 103, 105; "The Eve of St. Agnes," 29, 61, 97, 105, 113; "The Eve of Saint Mark," 61, 113; *The Fall of Hyperion*, 30–31, 60, 70; *Hyperion*, 29, 60, 67, 104; "Imitation of Spenser," 26; *Isabella*, 33, 69, 90; *King Stephen*, 104; "La Belle Dame Sans Merci," 30, 61, 104; *Lamia*, 30, 97; "Ode to a Nightingale," 41; "Ode to Apollo," 26; "On First Looking Into Chapman's Homer," 87; "On Seeing a Lock of Milton's Hair," 27; "Sleep and Poetry," 26–27, 40, 97, 101; "To Byron," 26; "To Chatterton," 26; "Written in Disgust of Vulgar Superstition," 33
Keats, Tom, 20, 22, 29, 41, 52

Lamb, Charles, 90
Landor, Walter Savage, 38, 48
Lockhart, John Gibson, 7, 12–14, 42–43, 45, 102; *Life of Scott*, 12–14
Lowell, Amy, 2, 3, 91, 95–107, 110; on *Endymion*, 27, 101–2, 103–4; on Keats's letters to Fanny Brawne, 16, 104, 106; on psychology, 98–99; "To John Keats," 95
Lowell, James Russell, 47–48, 66, 72
Lyons, John O., 6

MacCarthy, Desmond, 94
Manchester, William, 117n.15
Masefield, John, 3
Mason, William, *Life of Gray*, 6, 9, 13, 42, 48
Mathew, George Felton, 25, 26
Matthews, G. M., 2
Mendelson, Edward, 117n.15
Milnes, Richard Monckton (Lord Houghton), 5, 37–57, 62, 63, 75, 110; Fanny Brawne, treatment of, 50–51, 64; on Keats's illness, 64–65; on Keats's origins, 47–48; on Keats's religion, 51–52; letters and poems by Keats, use of, 18, 25, 43, 49–57, 85; *Life of Keats*, 16, 37, 38–57, 59–60, 82; *Poetical Works of Keats* (1876), 60; on social and sexual propriety, 54–57
Moore, Thomas, 10–12, 14, 45–46, 64; *Life of Byron*, 10–12, 42–43, 48–49
Morley, John, 77, 87, 92
Moxon, Edward, 53, 67, 79
Murry, John Middleton, 29

Nelson, Horatio, Lord, 9–10, 46
New Criticism, the, 43
Newman, John Henry, Cardinal, 51
Nightingale, Florence, 38

Patmore, Coventry, 52, 55
Praz, Mario, 38, 56
Pre-Raphaelite Brotherhood, the, 46, 47, 61
Prothero, R. N., 88
Psychology in biography, 98–99, 110–11, 112. *See also* Freud, Sigmund

Rank, Otto, 110, 112
Reynolds, John Hamilton, 19, 28, 34
Rice, James, 22, 54, 85, 105
Richardson, Sir Benjamin Ward, 81
Rollins, Hyder Edward, *Keats and the Bostonians* (with Stephen Parrish), 98; *The Keats Circle*, 18, 33, 39, 109; *The Letters of John Keats*, 17, 53, 109
Rossetti, Dante Gabriel, 61–63, 65, 66, 72
Rossetti, William Michael, 48, 61, 75–76, 77, 78–82; on Keats's letters to Fanny Brawne, 79–81; *The Life of John Keats*, 78–82, 86; *The Poetical Works of John Keats*, 67

Scott, Sir Walter, 12–14, 43, 45, 100
Severn, Joseph, 39, 51–52, 60, 86, 103, 105
Shakespeare, William, 16, 61, 70, 72
Shaw, George Bernard, 32
Shelley, Percy Bysshe, 15, 46, 61, 63; *Adonais*, 40, 62, 65, 95; "Defence of Poetry," 46, 100

Sontag, Susan, 63–64
Southey, Robert, 7; *Life of Nelson*, 9–10, 45, 93
Stephen, Leslie, 77, 78
Stevenson, Robert Louis, 82, 83–84
Stillinger, Jack, 113
Strachey, Lytton, 42, 44, 96, 107; *Eminent Victorians*, 91–95, 104; on Victorian biography, 42, 44
Swinburne, Algernon Charles, 38; "In Sepulcretis," 67; view of Keats's letters to Fanny Brawne, 16, 66–69
Sympathy in biography, 99–100

Taylor, John, 34, 97
Tennyson, Alfred, Lord, 11, 37, 67, 78; "On Reading a Life and Letters," 67, 120n.7
Thompson, Francis, 65
Trilling, Lionel, 31

Ward, Aileen, 110–11, 112
Weller, Earle V., 17, 19
White, Newman Ivey, 94
Whitehead, Alfred North, 112
Wilde, Oscar, 73
Woodhouse, Richard, 83, 102, 109
Woolf, Virginia, 16, 42, 94
Wordsworth, William, 49, 119n.31; "Letter to a Friend of Robert Burns," 7–8, 25, 43, 119n.26; *The Prelude*, 15

Yeats, William Butler, 2, 91

OHIO UNIVERSITY LIBRARY

Please return this book as soon as you have finished fine it must be returned in order to avoid a stamped below.

RETURN BY

NOV 1 3 1986

RETURN BY

DEC 1 1986

NOV 1 7 1986

RETURN BY

MAR 2 9 1988

RETURN BY

MAY 1 2 1988

RETURN BY

NOV 2 7 1989

RETURN BY

MAR 2 9 1993

MAR 1 2 1993

APR 2 4 1997

APR 0 4 1997
CF